AUSTIN'S HARVEST

A Harvest of Forgiveness

Donna Lofthouse

Austin's Harvest:
A *Harvest of Forgiveness*

ISBN 979-8-218-02247-1

Lofthouse Publishing
Bradenton, Florida

Printed in the United States of America

Dedication

I DEDICATE THIS BOOK to my son Austin, who taught me how to have an open heart when it mattered the most, and to everyone his life touched whether through a personal relationship with him or through reading about his story and finding forgiveness and healing.

To my husband Dan for standing with me through the tears and the trials, and always supporting and believing in me.

To my son Chris whose courage and wisdom greatly surpassed my expectations, to Keila for loving him so well and teaching him to laugh again.

To my daughter Hannah who has such a beautiful pure heart and maturity beyond her years, I have enjoyed becoming her best friend!

To my whole family who allowed me the freedom to walk in forgiveness and love and never questioning the motives of my heart.

To my best friend Dawn who walked me through those dark places and into the light. You let me just cry when I needed to cry, prayed with me when I needed to pray. You showed up that devastating night and interceded with me for hours for God's perfect will to be done.

To Jennifer, who worked alongside of me and knew exactly what I was going through.

To every one of my friends who stood by my side and continually lifted us all up in prayer every step of the way.

I also dedicate this book to every one of Austin's Best Friends, there were so many! You know who you are! You all gave Austin an opportunity to show the world his beautiful smile and selfless heart!

I also dedicate this book to someone whose courage and strength and humility have far surpassed anyone that I will possibly ever meet in my lifetime, Alex. I know that God has amazing plans for your life. I know that one day when you are ready, you will be able to give your testimony and as you speak, hearts will listen to what you have to say, and many people will be healed, delivered and set free. You have paid a great price that only you and God truly know, I am grateful that you allowed me to walk by your side through it all and didn't push me away. I dedicate this book to your family as well, your mom Katrina, who kept me balanced and encouraged through our many talks tears and prayers. Your dad Lane, who was the first of Austin's harvest to accept the Lord Jesus into his heart and life just days after the accident. Whom always kept me informed, encouraged and sat by my side through the heartbreaking trial.

To my Door, church, and Healing Rooms family that ministered healing to us all and interceded every step of the way.

I especially dedicate this book to everyone in Austin's family or friends that didn't understand why I did what I did when I stood in the place of forgiveness, I pray that as you read this book you will have clarity into my choices and decisions. I pray that it will honor you, and honor Austin's memory in such a way that it will become a blueprint for others to follow that may bring healing and restoration to the brokenhearted and set captives free.

I am also thankful for the late nights spent in the beautiful cabin of the Blue Ridge Mountains editing this book with Theresa, Diana and Ashley. You laughed and cried with me. I was truly touched when you each shared with me that you felt like you knew Austin even though you had never met.

To my sisters, Ina, Susan and Mary, thank you for your encouragement as we all sat together and read Austin's Harvest together in Koh Samui Thailand.

I would like to thank Jane for your creative editing and bringing this book to life through your direction and expertise, I could not have done this without you.

Acknowledgements

I WANT TO THANK Jesus Christ my Lord and Savior. Without you loving me and guiding me every step of the way, I would have quickly fallen apart and isolated myself in brokenness and it would have been impossible for the turn of events to take place that will play out in this book.

Scriptures upon which to build your faith

John 3:16 (NIV)

[16] For God so loved the world that he gave his one and only Son, that whoever believes in him shall not perish but have eternal life.

Romans 10:8-10 (NIV)

[8] But what does it say? "The word is near you; it is in your mouth and in your heart," that is, the message concerning faith that we proclaim: [9] If you declare with your mouth, "Jesus is Lord," and believe in

your heart that God raised him from the dead, you will be saved. [10] For it is with your heart that you believe and are justified, and it is with your mouth that you profess your faith and are saved.

Colossians 1:13-24 (NIV)

[13] For he has rescued us from the dominion of darkness and brought us into the kingdom of the Son he loves, [14] in whom we have redemption, the forgiveness of sins.

[15] The Son is the image of the invisible God, the firstborn over all creation. [16] For in him all things were created: things in heaven and on earth, visible and invisible, whether thrones or powers or rulers or authorities; all things have been created through him and for him. [17] He is before all things, and in him all things hold together. [18] And he is the head of the body, the church; he is the beginning and the firstborn from among the dead, so that in everything he might have the supremacy. [19] For God was pleased to have all his fullness dwell in him, [20] and through him to reconcile to himself all things, whether things on earth or things in heaven, by making peace through his blood, shed on the cross.

[21] Once you were alienated from God and were enemies in your minds because of your evil behavior. [22] But now he has reconciled you by Christ's physical body through death to present you holy in his sight, without blemish and free from accusation— [23] if you continue in your faith, established and firm, and do not move from the hope held out in the gospel. This is the gospel that you heard and that has been proclaimed to every creature under heaven, and of which I, Paul, have become a servant.

[24] Now I rejoice in what I am suffering for you, and I fill up in my flesh what is still lacking in regard to Christ's afflictions, for the sake of his body, which is the church.

Ephesians 1:7 (NIV)

[7] In him we have redemption through his blood, the forgiveness of sins, in accordance with the riches of God's grace

Romans 8:2 (NIV)

[2] because through Christ Jesus the law of the Spirit who gives life has set you[a] free from the law of sin and death.

2 Corinthians 5:17 (NIV)

[17] Therefore, if anyone is in Christ, the new creation has come: The old has gone, the new is here!

Contents

Introduction

As I was sitting in a familiar church attending the funeral service of a young shooting victim, I began to reflect upon my own parallel path. It must have been the News Cameraman in the parking lot I had just passed by that triggered the memories as they began to flood my mind. The most impactful one was the day before the trial of my son Austin's best friend, Alex. That day, in this very parking lot, I sat in my car for a while before I walked in. I could hear the worship music echo from the walls of the church as I spoke with Alex's dad, Lane, on the phone. He was being transparent and sharing the information with me that he had just received from his son's attorney, Mac, so we could prepare for the difficult week ahead.

At that time, I had been fasting, praying, and trusting that God was in perfect control. After I found a seat that day, I listened to the timely message followed by communion and a call to the altar for prayer. I was drawn to the front and received a word of encouragement. What was spoken over me was so profound that I felt it penetrate my heart. The Minister said that the Holy Spirit was showing her that I was a living epistle and that I had drank from a cup that not many would choose.

I didn't really know what that meant yet, but I felt it and I received it.

I looked up the meaning on biblehub.org, and this is what I found:

[2]You yourselves are our letter, written on our hearts, known and read by everyone. [3]You show that you are a letter from Christ, the result of our ministry, written not with ink but with the Spirit of the living God, not on tablets of stone but on tablets of human hearts. 2 Corinthians 3:2-3 (NIV)

What was the cup that not too many would choose to drink from? Simply put, it was walking in forgiveness and love. It is not only to forgive, but it is to walk it out and live it before the world.

The scarf bore the image of a dark skin dancer on it. When we go to Cuba, we stayed with a couple in Havana, Des and Glory, little did we know how very instrumental they would become in our visits there. When we first met, I asked Glory what she did for a living, she told me that she was a dancer. She looked exactly like the dancer on the piece of silk that I had created with long black dread braids and full of grace and strength! I knew then it was created just for her.

The following year we met in Cuba again and I was honored to lead her in the prayer of salvation as she accepted Jesus into her heart as her Lord and Savior (Just a couple of months before, her husband had done the same with a group from our church). I was surprised when she called me forward to the front of the Cuban church we were visiting and honored me with a dedicated worship dance using the billowing silk dancer piece that I had painted for her the year before. She shared with the church that she couldn't believe that there was a God that loved her so much that He would have someone make this for her and bring it to her before we ever met!

All of these memories bring me back to a time a few years ago when we went through the most difficult trial of our lives. Without God leading us every step of the way, without his grace, his mercy and his love, it would have been impossible for any of us to make it through the long journey ahead and ultimately through the process of healing. I don't know how people get through difficult times without Him. Jesus was the glue that held me together.

My family, friends, and I walked through the fire so to speak, a time of Fasting, prayer, purification and testing of the very character and intent of our hearts. I was so blessed and loved as family and friends had come up alongside me and we walked it out together. Looking back now, I learned something that was so profound that it gave me a whole new perspective of the mother's role in the family. *The mother is the thermometer of the family.* I learned that if I stayed focused and steadfast, then everyone else would be able to follow my lead. I had to be the strongest one. If they saw me fall apart then they would all fall apart, too. Wow!

I've never been a writer, or one that enjoyed reading, in fact I never would have believed that I would live a life that was beyond ordinary, and someday become an author. The reason that I started to journal through each day was when I began to realize there seemed to be a profound orchestration in the details of my life. I knew that what I was walking out needed to be recorded. I remember saying over and over you just can't make this stuff up! Or, this is a well written, orchestrated script for a movie! When things seem to divinely fall together like pieces to a puzzle you begin to see the big picture, God's hands were all over the details, and it got my attention! I invite you into the script of Austin's Harvest!

Chapter 1

The Gun Show

WHILE ROUTINELY GOING ABOUT my life, I thought that I had it all somewhat figured out. Living a Spirit filled life as a wife and mother, serving in church and ministry, always giving to those in need within my realm of influence. I can recall the different seasons I had walked through, like helping single moms, even picking up their children for church on Wednesday nights and Sunday mornings. On two separate occasions I had calls from young mothers and asked if I could bring them to the hospital and help them through their deliveries, what an honor and joy that was. It seemed like I was doing all the right things! One Tuesday morning after worship and prayer, I was ministering at the Healing Rooms and as we usually do, we were broken up into teams of three for each of the three rooms. Earlier that morning, I had what seemed like a supernatural experience, I was awakened in the middle of the night to something odd that I had never experienced before. It felt surreal in my bedroom. As always, my husband Dan was sleeping peacefully, he could and has slept through a hurricane! So, I sat up in bed as I do whenever I wake up in the middle of the night and glanced over at the clock beneath the TV to see what time it was. All I could see was a blurry, bright light. It was a bit hazy throughout the room like there was a heavy glory cloud in the room! Even the alarm clock on my nightstand was impossible to read, it too was red and blurry. Weird, I thought.... I don't normally have such blurred vision. I discounted it at the time and fell back into a very deep sleep.

As I shared this strange occurrence with my prayer team members it was quickly dismissed and forgotten. That day our team had the privilege of praying for one of the new directors of another Healing Rooms in Northern Florida. Since each session is confidential, I am only going to share the Scripture spoken and what was said to me.

When it was my opportunity, I walked around to pray for the gentleman. The Holy Spirit gave me just one Scripture and a simple word, which for me, would soon become profound. It was Mark 12:30-31 (NIV):

> [30]And you shall love the Lord your God with all you heart, and with all your soul, and with all your mind, and with all your strength. [31]The second is this, you shall love your neighbor as yourself. There is no other commandment greater than these.

So, I spoke that Scripture over him, and as I was about to walk away, he said something to me that I was not expecting. He said he was seeing something that he wanted to share with my permission.

Usually, the model we follow doesn't allow the one receiving prayer to minister to the team members, but because he was a director, it was allowed, and I welcomed the edifying word he had for me.

He said that while I had been looking into his eyes and ministering the word of God to him, he saw what looked like liquid fire swirling around in my eyes. He told me that he had only seen this twice before, first in the eyes of Kenneth Hagin and then in the eyes of Kenneth Copeland. I said, "Wow, thank you," and although I didn't feel or see anything myself, I believe it was shown to him by the Lord for a purpose.

I have never forgotten that. Since that day I have had two people on two separate occasions tell me that they had seen fire swirling in my eyes, one during worship on a mission trip to Cuba, then again shortly after we had returned back home. I felt like it had something to do with being woken up that night before when I saw a hazy cloud in my bedroom. Considering the events that were getting ready to unfold, I believe it was God preparing me to walk through the fire. That Scripture was a truth not only for him, but it was burning into my heart as well.

The Healing Rooms is wonderful place to volunteer and train if you have a heart to help people in their healing process, also to develop your spiritual gifts. Rooted and grounded in the Word of God the seasoned team members represent many different Christ centered denominations which are accountable to leadership. It's a wonderful place to go for prayer, to call upon the Lord for your specific need—emotional or physical healing or spiritual strengthening. You can truly feel the presence of God when He is invited into your circumstances—May His will be done on earth as it is in Heaven.

We all need to have faith in this difficult world and stay grounded in His Word. When we believe and agree with who he says we are, and as we yield our life to his leading, we can experience his best for our life. I know for a fact that the past 13 years I've spent there praying for people at the Healing Rooms has strengthened me, my faith, and my trust in God. Becoming a trainer gave me the confidence that I otherwise, never would have had. Did I ever sit in my car in the parking lot telling myself that I was not qualified to be there? Yes! All the time! However, I felt strongly led by the Holy Spirit and obediently continued to go every week to be molded by God like a plain, ordinary lump of clay. He had to shape me and mold me into His unique vessel. I knew deep down within me that there was something more than what I could see, I can't even explain it. I knew that isolation would not take me to where I needed to go and become and who God created me to be. I knew that it was not just about being a wife and mother, or even a hairdresser, but that I was created to do great things.

There was a time that I recall, sitting in my car in the parking lot for 20 minutes battling with the spirit of rejection, trying to convince myself that I didn't belong there, plagued by thoughts that told me that I was not gifted like they were, that I couldn't be used by God, that I was weak, and that I didn't know the word of God well enough. I thought I should go home before they noticed me sitting out there in my car. Then, I just took a deep breath, picked up my Bible, stepped out of my car, and headed in through the front door. I was welcomed with the love of Christ by those inside, the very same people who were to stand by my side and prayed me through the trial soon to come.

The following Friday, three days after praying for that director, my older son Chris decided to come into town for the weekend, something that he never does. He's kind of a workaholic, and constantly works to reach the goals that he sets for himself. It turned out that one of his friends had asked him to make the long 250-mile drive with her so she could meet her sisters' new baby, just 45 minutes North of where we live. She planned on dropping him off for the weekend visit and returning home on Sunday afternoon. She didn't like driving long distances alone since the year before she had been in a serious and tragic accident.

He knew that she wanted to see her sister and the new baby and that she didn't want to make the long drive by herself. So, he did something that he normally would never do. He called off work and came home Friday afternoon for a three-day weekend that had been long overdue.

My younger son, Austin, met them at a designated place near the interstate and picked up Chris. As I look back, I can see that God had blessed them with this time together. They were always happy to be with each other. They loved to do everything together. At 22 and 26 years of age, they got along well. They certainly took every opportunity to drive me crazy, like putting on those pink boxing gloves and having a match in the front yard or singing impromptu rap songs in sync like they had practiced for hours. They just finished each other's sentences. They loved each other and were best friends. I don't know how, but mothers seem to feel the bonds their children have with one another.

They hung out at Austin's and his roommate Alex's apartment that Friday night, then Austin brought Chris back home to our house where a room was kept when he came into town for a visit. We had recently surprised him by painting his walls blue and brown. Austin had come over with his tools and mounted a TV on his brother's wall.

It was all a big improvement from the pink and green wall with a bunny family mural that I had painted there years before for their 10-year-old sister, Hannah. Chris had told me that he was having nightmares of the bunnies attacking him at night and would occasionally wake up feeling like they were looking at him. He was telling me that they were evil little bunnies! So, I took the hint and while he was gone two months earlier, we had re-modeled his room—I had been watching too much home improvement tv, I must admit.

I remember that Austin had come over that night for the delicious dinner I had promised to serve him and afterwards we went into Chris' room to finish mounting the TV on the wall.

The one thing that I will never forget was what he brought with him that day when he came to install the TV for his brother—his new Smith and Wesson revolver. It was silver and he had it tucked into the front of his shorts. He wanted to show it to me. I didn't like it, and I remember being mad at him for bringing it to my house, especially with Hannah there. I made him put it in the closet until he was finished helping me.

Well, it was an opportunity for me to tell him that they are very dangerous, and that he needed to be very careful with it. He assured me that he would. I told him that he was mature enough to be living on his own and that I was sure he would be careful with the gun. When he finished working in Chris' bedroom, he said he was going to head home. I thanked him, kissed him on the cheek, gave him a hug, and out the front door he went. As he walked down the sidewalk, I said to him, "Hey Austin, are you forgetting something?" He turned around and said, "What?" Then he remembered that he had left his gun in the closet. "Oh, yeah!" he said, then went in and got it. In a minute he was off toward his apartment.

Earlier in the week, Austin's roommate, Alex, had just celebrated his 22nd birthday and planned on spending that week with his parents and sister Ruthie in Georgia. After he returned from that trip, they picked right back up where they had left off, playing their guitars and video games and just hanging out together.

The following day was Saturday, Chris, Austin, Alex and a couple of other friends hung out together. They went out to a popular sports bar and got a bite to eat and watched Hockey finals.

When they had stopped back by our house for Chris to change his shirt, Austin gave Hannah a big hug and said, "I love you!" They were off in a big hurry to meet their friend Jared at their apartment and head out to a gun show at the Convention center. They got a late start, so by the time they got there, it was near closing time. They split up in two's and walked around, checking out what looked interesting, Austin with Chris and Alex with Jared. Alex saw an accessory for his new Glock gun that caught his eye. It was a flashlight that mounted on the gun just in front of the trigger. It had different colored lenses that you could change for a different effect. He purchased it and looked forward to mounting it on his gun. As the gun show was closing for the day, the boys met at the exit and enjoyed their time together, so they carried their purchases in brown paper bags out to the truck.

They all piled into Jared's big red truck and went across the street to eat at a local burger restaurant. As usual, Chris and Austin acted like a couple of goofballs, having fun as they took the opportunity to embarrass their friends with their normal brotherly antics. As they headed home, Chris and Austin sat in the back seat and continued to show their manliness by having a fist fight to see who could deliver the best shot. Alex decided to capture this craziness and caught this show of affection on video, recording the brotherly love as they went at it. They quickly called a truce and acknowledged each other for their great hits and surprise punches, celebrating as brothers do with normal brotherly behavior.

Chapter 2
Grace Arrives

My husband Dan, Hannah and I were enjoying a Saturday night dinner at a local restaurant where Hannah was finishing up a large spin of cotton candy as a finish to her meal. (Whoever thought it would be a great idea to serve cotton candy in a restaurant for dessert!)

After we left the restaurant, we headed to the local Christian bookstore to pick up a birthday card for Chris, he was planning on leaving the next day to go back home after his visit with us. As we were standing at the register, my husband picked up Billy Graham's video, *My Hope America*, and added it to our purchase.

Once home we settled in for the night. Immediately upon walking in the door we were greeted by Max, our black Labrador and our chocolate Lab Ruby. Chris had blessed us with these two when he had taken a short-lived job in New York.

A few minutes had passed when the home phone rang at the exact same time that I was trying to call Chris on my cell. As I answered, I was quickly disconnected because his battery died on his phone. He called back from a different phone number, one that said Georgia on the caller ID. As I answered, my life changed right before my very eyes. Nothing would ever be the same again.

My son's voice gave me the message no mother ever wants to hear: *Mom, Austin's been in an accident and you need to come to his apartment as fast as you can. He's hurt really bad; you have to come now.*

"What kind of accident?" I asked him, but he wouldn't tell me.

"Mom, I have to go. The police are here now. Just come now," was his only response.

As I hung up the phone, I felt myself go numb. I told Dan to stay with Hannah and I would let them know what had happened. Then I got into my car and began to pray as I drove as fast as I could. That was when the prayer warrior in me came out. I began to pray in my prayer language—thank You, Lord, for the baptism of the Holy Spirit.

I began praying in tongues at the top of my lungs, and with as much authority as I could gain, I spoke decrees over Austin that he would live and not die. I spoke life, health, and healing over him. I continued to pray as I pulled up to the red light near his apartment.

I watched to my left as a fire truck followed by an EMS vehicle pulled out. I knew when they didn't have their lights on that Austin was gone—I just knew. I looked to my right and saw the high school football field where Chris used to play. Quickly, the memory popped into my mind of Austin walking so proudly beside Chris at his homecoming football game wearing his big brother's #17 "away" jersey. Oh, how Austin looked up to his big brother!

The light changed and I continued to pray as I contemplated in my beating heart of all that I was about to learn. I pulled into the apartment complex and flew over the speed bumps. It was around 8:35 pm. Sheriff cars with their flashing lights were everywhere. Yellow crime scene tape was being stretched out before my eyes. I pulled up so fast and threw my car into park that I forgot to turn off the engine. I saw Chris and ran to him. He was devastated. He had to tell me that Austin had died.

"He's gone! Chris cried, mom, Austin is gone. I tried mom, we tried to save him – he fought so hard.

He had told Austin to hang on and fight, he fought for every breath until he breathed his last. Chris said, "he had put his hand on Austin's heart and felt that it had stopped beating."" Those words hung in the air. I'm not even sure what all was said beyond that point. I had felt something come over me the moment I stepped out of the car. A blanket of God's grace covered me. It was as though I was standing beside myself and the Holy Spirit that abides in me took over. He led me. He guided me. He spoke and ministered through me. I was fully yielded to Him. It was like I had checked out and He had checked in. I prayed for Chris and held him. Chris had later told me that Austin didn't have any fear in his eyes as he passed, he was peaceful not terrified- he had peaceful eyes.

I looked around me and noticed the three young men before me- one standing -one sitting- and one on his hands and knees, all three visibly shaken and distraught. I was moved with compassion at that very moment. Jared was sitting at the foot of the stairs near Austin and Alex's apartment door as I approached him, he slowly looked up at me with such sorrow and unbelief. As he sat there, covered from head to toe in my son's blood, he looked at me and said, "I'm sorry. I'm so sorry. I tried to save him, but I couldn't. I held a towel over his wound, but I couldn't stop the bleeding."

"I know, Jared. It's ok," I said. "I know you did everything you could." He was in a state of shock. I asked him if I could pray for him and he said yes. I put my hand on his arm, knowing that Austin's blood had dried there, and I prayed for Jared. It reminded me at that moment of Jesus' blood that was shed for us, that covers us, and what it accomplished for us on the cross. I was eternally thankful that Austin had found his way, through the blood of Jesus, to the Father in Heaven. He walked through that eternal door and was now walking the streets of gold, and I would see him again one day when my destiny is fulfilled.

As I finished praying for Jared to have peace and healing from the trauma that he had experienced, I looked to my right and saw Alex, Austin's best friend. The two of them had been inseparable. They did everything together. They played guitar for hours every day and loved each other like brothers. There he was on his hands and knees on the concrete sidewalk, holding his head in his hands, rocking back and forth, I heard him saying over and over, "I'm so sorry. I'm so sorry. It was an accident; I can never forgive myself."

Suddenly I remembered what Chris had just told me, "Mom, Alex shot Austin and he's gone, Mom." This boy in agonizing sorrow before me was the one who had accidentally shot my son. It was a surreal moment. Time stopped. I felt myself moved with compassion for this young man. Without hesitation I got down on my knees next to him, and I put my arms around him and said, "Hey, Alex, it's Donna, Austin's mom."

He kept repeating "I'm so sorry, I can never forgive myself."

I gently said, "Listen Alex, I forgive you, and I know that Austin would forgive you. You have to forgive yourself." Then I told him with all my heart, "Alex, I love you." I placed my hand on his back and I began to pray for Gods peace to fill him at that moment I could feel Gods presence and I could feel the love and peace released to him. I asked him to give me a hug, and he got up on his knees and hugged me.

After a while I stood up and began to look around. The three boys were in their designated spots with a sheriff's detective standing by each of them. It was quiet and eerie. As I stood there, I didn't know who to call first. I didn't want to tell anyone over the phone what had just happened. I didn't want to believe it myself. Everything still felt so surreal.

Finally, I decided to reach out and call my best friend Dawn. She was out with her family at a restaurant downtown, Obrick's, celebrating her sons return from The Dream Center in California. When I told her what had happened, she took a cab and arrived as fast as she could. She was with me for the rest of the night. We continued to pray together throughout the ordeal.

Austin's and Chris' father arrived, and he was devastated. I remember him saying over and over, "This is the worst day of my life." He and Chris both let me pray with them. At one point I asked him if he had Jesus in his heart because I knew that he was going to need Him to get through this. Chris leaned over and gave me a little kick in the leg for asking such a question, but his dad responded with a yes. I was glad he responded that way.

A little later as I was standing alone, I felt two hands on my shoulders. They abruptly turned me around. It was him again. He was distraught and just hugged me for the first time in so many years- as he did, he had something to say so he said it. For what seemed like several long minutes he gave me all the credit for raising Chris and Austin. He said the only reason they turned out as well as they did was because of how I had raised them.

I felt like he had a chance at that moment, to tell me everything he had ever wanted to say but couldn't until that time. It all came pouring out. I felt very humbled by his compliments and appreciation, and I knew that I had to let him say everything he needed to say. But the truth is, it took two sets of loving parents to raise these boys. We are not perfect, but we did the best we knew how to do.

It was such a comfort to have Dawn standing close by praying with me.

I was lost in time. At some point, I noticed that I needed to go back to the car to recharge my cell phone because the battery was very low. As I approached the car, I realized that I had never turned off the engine. After two hours it was still running and hot!

While charging my phone, I discovered a text from my sister Susan in Maine asking me if everything was ok. She must have felt in her spirit that something was wrong. I didn't respond. I couldn't. I just wasn't ready to talk to my family yet.

I called my friend at the Healing Rooms to tell her what had happened. She prayed with me and wanted to come, but I told her no. Then I hung up and called another friend, Cara, who is an evangelist. She was on a cruise with her family somewhere in the Caribbean and was surprised that her phone had rung or that it had worked at all. She prayed for me, too.

I had barely hung up from talking with her when my phone rang. It was Dan. I knew I was avoiding this call, but I also knew I had to answer. He asked what was going on. In that moment I began to face the reality that this had actually happened, and I told him quietly, "Austin is not with us anymore."

"What? What? No. You're kidding me. What?" he said, shock in his voice.

"Don't tell anyone yet. Wait," I said.

We hung up and now the process had begun. The phone calls, having to tell everyone who loved my son, that he was gone; it was all so unfathomable. Where do you begin? How do you endure the pain and grief?

When I returned to the scene from the car, the detectives were continuing with their investigation, calling each of the boys into the police vehicle to be questioned. Dawn and I prayed and interceded during this process, for the accounts from each one to line up without contradictions. We prayed the detectives would find that this was truly a terrible, tragic accident and that no arrests would be made.

During that time there was a man who had shown up wearing a baseball cap. He had been talking to the detectives and seemed to know them. His name was Mac and would soon become Alex' attorney. Lane, Alex' dad, was in Georgia and didn't know who to call when he learned about the devastating news, and in that desperate moment he recalled that he knew one attorney that had been his daughter Ruthies soccer coach and happened to have his phone number securely stored in his contacts. That must have been a God thing. After a while the detectives returned from the van with their decision not to make any arrests, or press any charges finding it to be a tragic, horrible accident, all were all free to go.

Just then a car pulled up and parked. Two women got out of the car and walked toward us. They were stricken by what they were seeing, and I knew who they were right away even though I had never met them. Austin had talked about them all the time. They were a mother and daughter who lived upstairs. Sarah was the mom that often cooked for the boys and was there if they needed anything. Her daughter Jules was my son's new girlfriend. She was standing there, so beautiful! I could see how Austin would fall in love with her. (He had finally asked her out around Mother's Day, while I was in New York. The month before he moved to Heaven, he had found the courage to ask her out—my Mother's Day gift—an answered prayer!)

The two of them stood there devastated and in shock as I told them what had just happened. I hugged them and prayed with them; then they went upstairs to process what they had just learned. Later they came down with some water for us to drink while everything was being completed.

At long last, just before midnight the investigation was over, and we were free to go. The detectives were waiting for the coroner to come, and the boys had been invited by Sarah to go upstairs to get cleaned up. I looked at the far end of the parking lot and saw Alex sitting on the curb, still in shock. He was so broken. Before leaving, I walked over to him and sat down. I gave him my phone number and he nervously stored it in his phone. I asked him to call me if he needed to and told him again that I loved him. Then I gave him a hug goodbye before we left, and I told him that everything was going to be okay.

Chapter 3

The Harvest Begins

EARLIER THAT FATEFUL NIGHT while sitting on a flight of stairs opposite of Austin's building, catching my breath and waiting for Dawn to arrive, my mind began racing with memories and thoughts as if puzzle pieces were beginning to fit together. Suddenly, I heard in my spirit "Remember the bird; remember the cat." What was that about, I thought! I began sifting through a recent series of events and wondered why I was thinking about them at that time, now I understand why.

Recent losses that our family had gone through were flying through my mind. First, a few weeks before Easter, Dan had called me at work and was clearly upset. He had just witnessed our little yellow Cockatiel, Baby Bird, take her last breath. That was during the time of Lent. Emotions began to stir at our loss, and Hannah was told that her bird was flying around in Heaven now. She decorated the shoe box with her duct tape collection, and we headed to my parents' house for an emotional burial ceremony in their yard.

Then on Easter Sunday our cat, Caesar, (the best cat in the world) went missing. It was on the Monday after Easter that I was on my back-porch painting on silk when I heard a voice, and a strong impression that said, "Go walk along the lake and look for Caesar." I immediately got up and went out through the gate to begin walking and calling him. I stopped at the area where I came upon his remains. I can only describe it as a coyote attack, a more traumatic death than that of Baby Bird. I quickly went and got a shoe box and retrieved his remains, covered it up, and put it into a larger box so Hannah would think he had died of natural causes. She mourned and once again decorated a shoebox with her duct tape creations, and again we headed over to Nana's and Grandpa's house to lay him to rest.

Now I know that God had a way of preparing us and helping us through the grieving process of a much greater loss, preparation for losing Austin 50 days later, on Pentecost Sunday. Lent (the bird), Easter (the cat), and then Pentecost (Austin) speaks of the powerful story of the cross. (Lent) is a season of preparation for Christ's death and (Easter) His resurrection marks the end of the Easter season and now; "(Pentecost) the feast of weeks, the celebration of the beginning of the wheat Harvest" the giving of the Torah at Mount Sinai in Judaism and the day of the outpouring of the Holy Spirit in the upper room. Wow! It was only through God's mercy and his grace that he prepared us for the loss of Austin. It's especially evident today as we celebrate Rash Hashanah, the Jewish New year. You will see that I am always trying to connect the dots throughout this book and trying to uncover God's fingerprints, and what He is revealing to us through these puzzle pieces we call life and even through this tragedy.

As Chris, Dawn, and I were getting ready to leave, Chris went into Austin's truck and grabbed his brother's gray and white jacket and held it tight. Soon after we dropped Dawn off at her house, we pulled into our driveway around midnight, at the start of Pentecost Sunday. The process had begun and there was no turning back, this new alternate reality was beginning to unfold for all to see.

As we walked through the kitchen door we were greeted with tears and hugs from Dan, Hannah, and Dan's mom and dad, who had come over to comfort them. After they had gone home, we put our exhausted girl to bed and headed to our room. It was impossible to fall asleep that night. My heart was so heavy. About 2:30 am I heard the front door close. It was Chris's friend. I was glad he had someone to help comfort him. It was the longest night of my life.

I was reminded of a dream that I had a couple of months earlier. In the early morning hours just before waking I had dreamt that Austin had actually died, and we were all going through the acknowledgement stage. I remember that it had felt so real. After I had woken up, I quickly pushed the possibility away and forgot about it. After all, it was such a crazy thought.

Then, I remembered a couple of weeks after that dream as I was driving down the road and had an abrupt thought, "What if I lost one of my children? Would I be able to handle it? Would I be ok?" As I thought about it, I came to the realization that yes, I would; it would have to be yes. They all have received Jesus as their Savior, and I know where they would go—to Heaven.

I know that Austin is in Heaven and has been made perfect in the image of Christ. He is not dead, but alive in Christ. He is on the outside of our timeline, he stepped into Heaven's timeline, into eternity and we will see him again very soon. Now I must trust God because there is nothing that I can do about it.

Even though I had not slept all night, the morning came all too quickly for me. I went out on my back porch to my quiet place and sat in my chair. I sat there with my phone on my lap, waiting for the sun to come up, wondering who I needed to call first. I decided to call two friends that had already gone through this kind of loss themselves in hopes that they could help me understand and help pray me through this difficult process.

I kept calling my sister Mary, finally reaching her through her boy-friend's phone. Of course, she was devastated. We met at my parents' house and decided to all be there together when we told them.

Naturally, the first thing my parents did when we walked in was to start singing *Happy Birthday* to Chris. We had to quickly interrupt them before he started to cry. As soon as we told them what had happened, they each began to grieve. I had never heard my mother cry like that before. My dad just hung his head down and grieved quietly. I hugged them both and told them that I love them and they each said they love me, too.

Soon we left and went back home. I continued to make phone calls until each family member had been notified. All the while, I had been in constant prayer asking God, "What do I need to do next?" There were so many things that needed to be done, and by the grace of God, He was there walking me through each and every detail.

On Monday, I was sitting at home making the arrangements that needed to be completed for that day when Mary called me. She said, "they were all at the boy's apartment cleaning it out and that I should come down too." Alex' parents were there also cleaning out and pack-ing his things. She told me that I should come and speak to them. I didn't want to, but I got into my car and headed over there anyway.

There they all were in the apartment. Mary's boyfriend, John and friend Eric had gone in first. With a utility knife they had cut out the bloodied carpet in the hallway and washed down the walls so that the others could enter. It was very difficult for Chris to revisit the very spot where he had watched his brother take his last breath just two days earlier.

The same grace that had fallen upon me the night we lost Austin was still present upon me (and is to this day). Alex's parents reluctantly came out of his room to greet and hug me. They had no idea how I was going to react to them. Would I be angry? Distraught? Bitter? They wouldn't know until I had spoken with them.

The three of us stepped outside the door of apartment # 17 to talk and pray together. That's where our real friendship began. I became the friend Katrina wished she never had, because of what it now represented. We realized that we needed each other to get through this thing. Both families were hurting. They loved Austin very much, too.

So right there at that moment, Lane, Katrina's husband, shared with me, his mother was a Holocaust survivor, and he was not raised religiously. He continued, "I have never believed in God and I have lived my whole life as an agnostic. But I know that in the car last night all the way here, I felt something that I had never felt before. For the first time I felt God's presence."

I asked him if he wanted to give his life to Jesus and put his trust in God. His response was, "Yes, Donna, I do. I am ready to do that." So, there we were, Katrina, Lane, and I held hands and prayed together. His decision that day was the first salvation of many to come that I will call *Austin's Harvest*. Katrina had been praying twenty years for Lane to make this decision, and I am honored to have had a part in it.

Together as a group we continued to clean out the apartment. It was very emotional at times. We were all in a state of shock, but we knew that we needed to do this. At one point I saw a little folded piece of paper on the kitchen counter. When I realized what it was, I quickly kept it to myself—it was the tickertape from the night of the accident, recording the date, time, and Austin's faded vitals. I folded it back up and tucked it away in my wallet.

Sarah and Jules were upstairs in their apartment and came down to check on us from time to time. I wanted to give them something of Austin's to remember him by. I happened to be holding the framed Salvador Dali print that Alex had given Austin a couple of years earlier when his uncle had passed away. She and her daughter were Dali collectors, so it turned out to be the perfect keepsake for them.

Later I sat on the stairs making more phone calls—the same ones where Jared had sat a couple of nights before. From that spot I called my pastor and planned for the funeral service. I needed to make all the arrangements and I didn't know how, but every aspect of the planning fit together like a puzzle. Each day the pieces that I needed just fell in front of me and I put them together as He ordered each step. It wasn't me; it was God leading me.

Chapter 4

Austin's Harvest

ONE OF THE MOST comforting things that we have received through this tragedy is the love and friendship that I've had over the years with a sweet couple, Chuck and Diane. They have been my clients at the salon where I work for over 20 years. They are more than just my clients; they have become like family. Chuck works as a funeral director in our town and now I have become his client. He had met my son Austin on occasion, and surely felt like he had known him through our conversations over the years. I called Chuck and told him about our loss and asked him if he would care for Austin and prepare him for his burial. He was compassionate and graciously took care of our every need. I can't even begin to tell you the peace that I had knowing that this man would do this with love, respect, and care. I have now come to understand in a greater capacity the impact that Chuck has made in this industry and for the countless families he has comforted. He lovingly prepares those entrusted to him with his best. He and Diane have the biggest hearts.

Austin had been hit in the neck by the bullet causing facial fractures. Chuck did an amazing job of reconstructing his jaw, although I had forgotten to ask him to leave the scar Austin had proudly displayed on his chin from the hockey puck that had landed there during a skate and shoot a couple of years back that he had attended with his brother. At the time, he had told me that the girls loved the one-inch scar across his chin! I wondered if anyone else noticed it was missing! Years later, when I had mentioned it to Chuck, he got all choked up and apologized for him not being perfect. I assured him that he was perfect, because it represented his body had been restored to perfection in heaven.

Austin was taken care of from the moment I had made the phone call to Chuck. The next step was to decide where the funeral service was to be held. I had never planned a funeral before, and I knew I was the one to complete every step so his dad wouldn't have to.

I called the office of the church that our family had recently left after years of attendance. The pastor answered the phone. He said that whatever we needed, anything that I wanted, he would do for me, so I asked him if we could use his sanctuary for the funeral service. He said *absolutely* and added that it would be at no cost to us as a blessing to our family. In my heart I had already known that was the place where we were to have it. Every time I closed my eyes and prayed, "Where God? Where are we supposed to have this service?" I saw in my mind it would be at this church.

With many memories of Austin at this church, I knew there was a purpose in returning. He had played his guitar in the youth group worship band years before, and then he moved out of town with his brother for a year. When he came back, he once again joined the worship team, but this time for the adult service.

A while back, after moving on from this church, both Austin and I had briefly carried the burden of offense. We had both been led to go back there to visit on occasion, even when we didn't feel like it. There were times when I didn't understand why I felt so uneasy, but I made myself get into the car and go. With a nagging feeling inside, I had to deal with my own heart. I was learning about forgiveness, time and time and time again. He knew what I didn't know—that I never would have been able to walk into that sanctuary for Austin's funeral service unless I had dealt with my own heart issues. He was also preparing my heart to forgive Alex immediately and I did.

Oh, the joy I had as a mother watching him up there on the platform playing his guitar so beautifully during worship, ushering in the presence of God. Now he is playing from the throne room of God for his Lord and Savior and King. I know that God is so blessed and pleased by his performance and love for Him.

Thursday, the day before the family viewing, Chris had invited all of Austin's friends to my house to "tell Austin stories" and encourage one another. Alex came that day, and while he was there, I invited him and their close friends to come to the family viewing. He said, "I wouldn't miss it."

It took a lot of courage for Alex to attend alongside our family at the viewing of his best friend whose life he had just taken. It was the most difficult thing to witness.

I carefully watched Alex throughout the viewing and stood close by him for support. As Austin's father spoke to him, friends and I stood near him as they exchanged words. I heard him tell this young man to do something great with his life for our son's sake. Alex said, "Yes sir. I promise I will." The boys all wore matching bracelets and I walked up to the casket with Alex and helped him put one on my son's wrist.

As I greeted some of Austin's family members, some had a puzzled look as if they didn't understand why I wasn't falling apart. I recognized it right away. I had seen it all throughout the week. I can't explain why I had such peace and strength. I just know that it came from God alone.

As we were leaving the family viewing, Hannah went to get into my sister's car. Her fiancé John was in the driver's seat. I said, "No, Hannah. They're not going where you and I are going." Just then he said, "I want to go where you are going," and I knew what he meant. So, I asked him if he wanted to invite Jesus into his heart and turn his life toward God. His answer was yes. So, we prayed right then and there, and he became the second agnostic man in a week to turn his heart toward God. Another seed was planted in Austin's harvest!

Earlier that same day, I needed a new pair of shoes, so my sister Ina and I headed to the mall. On the way, we made an unplanned stop by the church. At the moment we were getting out of the car, Chuck, the funeral director pulled up behind us as the pastor was walking through the parking lot. That's what I call perfect timing. God once again had gone before me guiding my every step.

After that short meeting we headed over to Macey's. I walked around the store in shock going through the motions of trying to purchase shoes for the funeral. As I was standing in line holding one shoe and waiting for help someone caught my eye. There was a beautiful woman that looked very familiar that had walked past me. Realizing it was Austin's stepmom, I spoke up and called out, "Is that you?"

Just then she looked over at me. She, too, looked in shock as she came over to me and we hugged for the first time ever. It was a surreal moment. All I could think to say was to ask her to forgive me for anything that I had ever said or done to offend her. She said the same to me then added, "I have wanted to call you and tell you how sorry I am. I have thought of you so often."

We made peace about four hours before we were to meet at the family viewing. It was God's grace at work once again. She was Chris and Austin's stepmom and we had lived in the same town for over 20 years and had never run into one another—ever. In His mercy and grace God allowed us to meet in private to honor one another and prepare for the difficult hours ahead. Shoes always have a way of bringing women together!

When I was at the funeral home earlier in the week choosing the dark mahogany casket, Chuck and Diane had a surprise for us. They wanted to purchase corner ornamental slides for the casket as a token of their love. I began to look through the catalog at all the choices. There were roses, crosses, flowers, praying hands, and then I came across the one that caught my eye—Harvest wheat. It was stalks of wheat standing in a bunch. It was bronze and golden wheat representing a harvest, Austin's Harvest.

All along, I had felt in my heart that Austin's death would reap a harvest of souls. And it is true that his story, in a unique way, has turned many hearts to the Lord and will continue to do so. Who he was as a person was so special. His friends describe him as selfless. He put others before himself always. He simply loved everyone. He had a way of making everyone he knew believe they were his best friend and a member of his family. He had a big heart; I know that it is because he had so long ago turned his heart over to Jesus.

Chris said that Austin was "the best Christian he had ever met, without telling you that he was one." He lived it. He had such joy all the time. Right after the accident, Chris also said in a newspaper interview, "If you put all of our family members together to form one body, Austin would be the smile." So yes, I will call all who come to the Lord through this story and our testimonies *Austin's Harvest*.

Chapter 5

I Want to Be Ready

SATURDAY MORNING CAME—THE DAY of the funeral. So, I got ready and headed out early. I brought Austin's guitars to the church and set them up on their stands, front and center, on the platform where he used to play. The flowers, mostly yellow roses and sunflowers began to arrive. There were so many beautiful centerpieces, one that had been made from a wicker guitar brought down from up North by his aunt Ina and uncle Steve. Large floral sprays were set up on each side of his guitars.

As I was taking the guitars out of their cases, I noticed that the strap on his black and white electric needed to be removed because it was not appropriate for the funeral. It was a yellow "police line do not cross" guitar strap that I had bought him for his birthday.

Ironically, my niece Corinne was graduating from high school and my nephew Jack was celebrating his fifteenth birthday the day that we lost Austin. The party they had planned to celebrate the following day was turned to sorrow as they all stood together to hold hands and lift us all up in prayer. That same day my nephew was given the very same guitar strap that I had just taken off Austin's guitar. I decided to give him this guitar to remember Austin by. I found out later that when he got home, without him even knowing about it, he had put his new strap on the guitar. It was meant to have that strap all along.

The worship team from our new church came to set up and practice the songs that I had chosen *I Can Only Imagine*, *I Will Rise*, and *I'll Fly Away*. There was another song that I had requested that totally caught them off guard—*I Want to Be Ready* by Fortress, a band from the 80's. My previous pastor happened to be in the original band as well as one of the worship members from my new church. They didn't miss a beat; it was meant to be. A song they had written decades ago, covered in dust until it brought them back together again, as they were reunited to play for the last song of the service. It was very fitting for Austin and everyone in attendance that loved electric guitars. Not only was it unforgettable, but it also reunited a couple of old friends.

Every detail was Spirit-led and fit together like a well-designed plan. My mother-in-law had done an amazing job of putting together a PowerPoint presentation of all the pictures of Austin and music of Journey. I had asked all his friends separately at the house earlier in the week what his favorite music was and they all said the same thing—Journey.

The open casket was placed in the back of the church between the two entrance doors so people could pay their respects and then be seated. The sanctuary and balcony held about 300 people. I had no idea how many people would come.

The grace of God was still heavy upon me and I couldn't believe that God had walked me through every detail almost alone. It was all Him because there is no way that I could've known what to do or how to do it.

The people finally began to fill the sanctuary. I had purposely saved two seats in the second row for my husband and I to sit with my family. I found myself completely composed greeting the multitudes of people that came to me. I began to realize just how much Austin had impacted the lives of the families there. As the sanctuary quickly filled up and the balcony as well, they began to bring in chairs from the fellowship hall and set them up in the back. It was standing room only. Wow! It was amazing to see how many people came to show their love.

I had kept the second row on the left open for Austin's closest friends. I didn't count the seats or even know how many there were, but as they came down the aisle together, there was such order. They all sat and exactly filled every seat.

As I watched Alex and his close friend Racheal follow behind them, I realized we needed two more seats. Remembering the two seats I had saved; I quickly had my family all move to the right. This opened the two seats directly behind me for both of them to sit.

I was close enough for Alex to draw on my strength if needed. Once again, he showed great courage, knowing that he was responsible for the grief of everyone in that church. I constantly encouraged him, as I knew he needed a reassuring look or a hug or just to tell him that everything is going to be ok. His family, along with Sarah and Jules were seated in the balcony and had a bird's eye view.

Austin's dad and stepmom, along with their family, sat along the right front row. The pastoral staff sat in the front left row. I had asked my current pastor to perform the ceremony, which he did with humility. He did a wonderful job of giving the message of salvation, without having an altar call. It's the Holy Spirit's job to convict and to draw hearts to Himself all in His perfect timing. I think Austin wouldn't want someone to feel uncomfortable at his expense.

There were a few people who came forward to speak. Chris went forward, turned to face the full sanctuary, and was astounded at how many people were there. He put his elbows on the music stand he stood behind. As he took a deep breath the weight of his arms gave way to the stand and it slid down as if Austin was playing a trick on him. He broke the ice as everyone began to laugh. He had some amazing words to say.

He was followed by his uncle who spoke on restoration and it being the theme of the funeral. Austin's dad and his family and my family had our friendship restored through this tragedy. We were all getting along for the first time in 20 years. There were some families in attendance that had left this church not thinking that they would ever walk back through the doors again, also showing forgiveness and restoration.

A couple of Austin's friends also came forward to speak. One shared about a time when Austin had encouraged him. He was looking for advice for his future and Austin had this to say: "*your future is like a large staircase and you can't see where the steps lead to, so you just take the first step that is in front of you, and then the next, and it will take you where it will lead you.*" If you only knew the great things that this young man has accomplished in his life since Austin told him that, then you would be astounded.

The service was just about over. It ended with I *Want to Be Ready* by Fortress. I had told the pastor's wife, that morning that I would be honored if she would sing the song with them. I could tell that she was happy to be a part of the closing song as she knew all the words by heart and is on the worship team at the church. I was blessed to hear her sing.

As we began to depart my best friend Dawn and I were hurried to my car to be the first car behind the hearse. The police escort was something! I know Austin would have been most proud of it, and I only hope that he could witness more than 300 people being led down the local streets by a police escort, blocking traffic at every light.

My brother had a coin that had Ephesians 6:10-18 written on it about the armor of God. It had been given to him by his wife. He had taken it to Iraq with him and kept it in his pocket during two of his many tours of duty. He asked that it be placed in Austin's pocket prior to burial. (Various friends and family had placed bracelets on his wrist, pins upon his shirt sleeve, an iPod and guitar picks in his pocket.)

As we all approached the hearse, Austin's closest friends were there, ready to carry him to his final resting place. As the pastor completed the final reading and before they began the process of lowering the casket, Chuck had removed the wheat harvest casket slides and presented the four keepsakes to me. I turned and looked at the boys and asked them to wait a moment before leaving. I handed a Harvest ornament each to Chris, Alex, Jared and Jon told them that the corners represent the harvest that will come to the Lord through Austin's life and through his death and through his testimony. I'm pretty sure at the time they didn't appreciate the full implications of what I was giving them, but I know one day they will look at them and understand.

Following the service there was a gathering at my mother- and father-in-law's house. The whole back porch was filled with the flower arrangements from the church. Alex's parents and all of Austin's friends had gone to his favorite dive downtown after the service because he loved to go there. All 14 of them ordered what he would have ordered—a double-cheeseburger with a cup of potato salad and a cold beer. Alex insisted he pay the bill for everyone's meal that day.

Chapter 6
A Moment in Time

THE FOLLOWING DAY MY sister Susan, her son Jack, and I drove to pick up all of the beautiful flower arrangements to donate them to a Hospice House. Of course, we used Austin's big red Ford F150 truck as the delivery van. As we arrived there, I saw a volunteer, an older client of mine George, that I've known for years. I had to ask him to sit down before I told him why I was there. He understood my loss and was very compassionate. He said he would make sure that the donated flowers would be made into bouquets and distributed to the sick and dying patients.

While we were there, we began to talk with a couple who were there with their daughter. She had been a drug addict living on the streets until being found and reunited with her mother and father just a week earlier. We asked if we could pray for her, and they said, "Yes, please." They were Christians, too. You could tell that she didn't have very much time left. I had anointed her head with oil, and we prayed for her. Then I asked her, if she saw Austin when she got to Heaven, to tell him that his mom said hi and that I miss and love him.

As I reflected on Austin's maturity, I was so amazed to see that he truly had his life and finances in order. He had his own little system that made me smile.In his apartment, he had his FPL envelope with payment enclosed, thumbtacked to the wall by the front door. I noticed that there were numerous tack holes on the wall suggesting that this is how he prepared and remembered to pay his bills on time every month!

When we had gone to the rental office to terminate his lease and turn in his keys, we found that he had fulfilled his lease for the year at the end of this month of June. When I went to pay his power bill, it was $0.95. His Bright House bill was $43. He had one credit card with a positive balance of $300 on it. He had perfect credit, no debt. Whatever he wanted he worked for, saved for, and bought it with cash. He had a savings account with $1,100 in it and he had just bought a red 2000 Ford F-150 truck with cash. He was so proud of that truck. He had even sold his old car to a man and taken a payment plan to help the guy out. I was so proud of Austin for having his financial house in order. More than that, he had his heart in perfect order and he always put others first throughout his life.

As I contemplate the time he had on this earth, I realize that Austin had quality time with everyone before he left! He made time for everyone. Here are just a few examples. He got to spend a lot of time with a childhood friend and first roommate Jon along with his brother Jake and sister Kate. These kids were all into music. Jake could play just about any instrument you gave him. I remember Austin had called him a genius. They each did their part in the worship team at church. They all went to elementary, middle and high school together and had a special bond. Kate counted Austin like a brother. That night at work she took the most difficult call that she could ever imagine as a 911 dispatcher; she was one of the first to learn of the tragedy that night. She had to call her parents to come and pick her up from work and waited until the entire family was all together at home before she shared the news. They all took the news quite hard as they felt as if they had lost their own son and brother.

Dan, Hannah, and I went to a Saturday night church service out east where quite a few friends attend. Dan, Hannah and I went to a Saturday night church service east of where we live, I purposely brought a gift for one of Austin's friends, Dave, whose mom regularly attends there. Dave had played the drums in their youth worship band, and I thought it only fitting that he be gifted Austin's set of wooden drumstick kitchen spoons that I had had given him the previous Christmas. She told me he would cherish them, thanked me for the gift and tucked them into her purse.. It was a set of wooden kitchen drumstick spoons that I had bought Austin for Christmas the previous year. He loved them.

I was surprised to see Jon come walking through the door! He had come to town to visit his parents that weekend. After church he asked if he could talk to me. Of course, I said yes. As we sat down, I could tell he was deeply troubled. He shared with me that he was sorry that he had made some bad choices in life and ended up moving out of his and Austin's apartment to work out of town in another state.

I told him that just because he moved out and Alex moved in and took his place as Austin's roommate, it didn't mean the accident was his fault. He started to cry and said he couldn't sleep at night and felt responsible for leaving Austin. He believed that if he hadn't left, then Austin would still be alive. I told him, even if he hadn't moved out, this still could have happened. *"It's not your fault,"* that was a comfort to him. He hugged me and said, "Thank you, Miss Donna. I feel so much better getting that off my chest."

When I told this young man that I didn't know what to do with Austin's truck, he lit up and said, "Please consider me, Miss Donna. I don't have a lot of money, but I would love that truck." I told him I would let him know.

It was a big day for Hannah, the first day of 6th grade at her new sclt was a big day for Hannah, the first day of 6th grade at her new school. It was bittersweet as I drove her there in Austin's red truck, she nervously got out and I took a few "first day of school pictures" of her standing next to it. It was an emotional milestone for both her and the truck. After sending her off with a kiss and a hug, I headed directly over to the tag office where I had arranged to meet Jon's mom and dad. As we were called up, I was surprised to see my friend Coco would be the one to walk us through the next step of transferring Austin's truck over to Jon's parents. She was deeply touched as she learned that I was gifting Jon the truck. Her husband Eric had been Austin's t-ball coach when he was just six years old and then his football coach for the next 6 years. His gift to us during this difficult time was the football jersey that sat on "Austin's table".

I spoke to Jon's dad in the parking lot and asked him if he knew where Austin was now. His answer was, "Yes, he's in Heaven." I asked him if he was ready to ask Jesus into his heart as one of Austin's harvest. He said, "When I'm ready to do that you'll be the first one that I will call." I'm sure one day I will receive that call.

Jon was so surprised to receive the truck and found the well-worn hat I had placed on the seat for him to find. I am convinced that he talked with Austin as he drove the truck around, and it helped him heal.

On Thanksgiving morning, Jon drove by to check on us and let us know how he was doing. As he was leaving, I told him that I had something for his brother Jake. I went into the other room and I came out with Austin's red Ibanez guitar that he had played in the youth group band in church.

He took the guitar home and hid it without telling his brother about it. When Thanksgiving dinner was on the table, the family each gave thanks one at a time. When it was Jakes turn, Jon told his brother to close his eyes because he had something else to be thankful for. Then he came around the corner with that guitar and told his brother to open his eyes. The look on his face was priceless. Their mom sent me the video—you know it's all about these kids. It really is—who they are going to become and how they are going to affect the world.

After graduating High school, Austin had gone to live and work with his brother Chris for about a year. They had some fun adventures and created some amazing memories together! After spending a year working for Chris, getting fired by Chris and rehired by Chris, it was time to head back home. Chris had another opportunity to move to Long Island NY, a short-lived adventure, but it brought Austin back home to live with me. His friend, Jared (from the night of the accident), had gone off to college and lived close to them. They spent a lot of time together too!

That's when Austin had a great opportunity to work with his dad and learn the trade of electrician. It was time well spent for both. For two years he learned responsibilities and how to use tools, but the most important thing that came from this time was father and son time that was so important to both of them. Memories were made, love was shown, respect was given, friendship was developed—what a gift. Each morning that his stepmom got to see him and start her day off with his smiling face—a gift. He and his dad going on a night-time bike ride—a joy. He always had time for everyone and seldom said no to anyone who asked him for help or anything.

He played hockey on a team that Chris and Dan had talked him into joining with them. They quickly became the "family line" on the ice. I could recognize them with their white helmets on, jumping out of the box in sequence onto the ice. It was something they did together, and they loved it.

Just two months before Austin went home to Heaven, Jared ran into one of their old friends. Justin had joined the Marines and was now home and wanting to see Austin. Jared gave him Austin's number and they met up.

In their conversation, Justin confessed to Austin, that he did something stupid one night. He told him that he was driving past his house and took the iPod from his car. As he apologized Austin said, "Man, is that all? That's high school stuff, dude! It's okay. I forgive you. I got a new one!"

Both needed that forgiveness before it was too late to ask for it. That's what you call God's grace. This young man was one of those who carried Austin's casket as a pallbearer; it was meant to be that they reconnected.

Every time I've gone out to Austin's grave to clean it up or water his plants, I've never known what to expect. There have been many trinkets left by family and friends. I have wondered on several occasions who was leaving the fresh flowers for him. One day as I was sitting on the bench praying, a young woman pulled up behind my car and got out. She had flowers, a vase, and a gallon jug of water. I watched and wondered who she was coming to visit. She walked right up to me and introduced herself. I thanked her for bringing flowers, and when I asked her what prompted her, she said, "He really impacted my life." Wow! What a blessing.

As we spoke, I told her that I didn't know what I would do without the Lord. She said that she would like to ask Jesus into her life and her heart, so we prayed. More harvest! What a beautiful and thoughtful young woman.

Chapter 7

A Time for Preparation

FOR THE FIRST TIME in 20 years the boys' dad, Dan, Chris and I went to have breakfast together one morning. What a miracle. Dan had been praying for years for their friendship to be restored. They were talking about old times and about Austin. It was true restoration.

Before their Sunday afternoon hockey game, Chris left with his dad to go visit Austin's grave then go kayaking. As always, Dan was ready early to get to the rink and practice. Jon came out to watch the game and we had a really good talk. He reminded me of the time that he bought his first gun while he was Austin's roommate. Before he could buy it from the private gun seller, he was required by the seller to complete a gun safety course. (That's the way it should always be.) He also told me that after we had spoken and prayed, he was feeling better about himself and sleeping all through the night.

Earlier in the month when Chris and I had driven down to his place in Fort Lauderdale together, we had a long three-and-a-half-hour drive for the purpose of bringing back Austin's truck to give to Jon. Chris was having the oil changed and serviced. After having breakfast together, Chris was off to work and I drove around in Austin's truck, eventually ending up back at Chris' apartment.

As I was cleaning, I saw Austin's wooden chest on Chris' dresser where he had kept his gun. I opened it up and noticed a box of rounds and a clip full of rounds. The sheriff's office had impounded his gun for evidence, and I had signed a waiver for it to be destroyed. So, what did I do now? I decided to take a bullet out of his clip and one out of the box and keep them as keepsakes. I put them both into the pocket of my wallet with the intention of putting them into my jewelry box when I got back home.

After that, I anointed Chris' apartment with oil and prayed throughout every room for God's peace and healing to flow through that place and for his safety and for the spirit of fear and trauma to leave him. It was time for healing for Chris, for Alex, and for all of us. Both Austin's and Alex's families were constantly covered in prayer. I found that I needed to speak to and pray with Alex's mom Katrina at least every two weeks or I had anxiety try to come upon me. As soon as we would pray together, I felt grounded, like I could make it through the pain and emotional highs and lows. We needed each other then and we still do today.

So, I got into Austin's truck and started the long drive home. By the time I pulled into my driveway I was totally exhausted. I immediately laid down to take a nap. As I finally fell into a deep peaceful sleep my phone rang. I jumped up and answered it. How I wished that call had never come.

It was from the State Attorney's Office. Two months had passed since the accident. The Sheriff's office had not pressed any charges in the case. It was homicide with a firearm. They didn't find it criminal, but a tragic accident. The only thing left was for the State Attorney's Office to look it over and to close the case.

The man on the phone introduced himself and told me that the case had been given to him. He went on to say that he had looked it over and had decided that there was enough evidence to prosecute, and that he was going to recommend prison time. My heart sank. I said, "My God, no!" Then I asked him how long this process might take, and he said it could take up to a year. He had already spoken to the Defense Attorney and told him that Alex needed to turn himself in. Then there would be a bail hearing and he could post bail.

I was speechless and horrified. This man was looking for an easy conviction; he said he thought he could get 30 years in prison. I pleaded with him not to do this. I told him that it was an accident and that I didn't want this. He didn't care what I thought. The mother of the victim had no voice. I said, "What if he would agree to become an advocate with my family and speak to the youth in schools and youth groups instead, or if he could go to the Dream Center in Los Angeles and complete a two-year court-ordered program and serve the needy and homeless on Skid Row?" Nothing. He didn't even listen to a word I said. He didn't care and he had already made up his mind.

After I regained my composure, I called Katrina and told her about my conversation with the State Attorney's office. This was the first she had even heard about it and it took her by surprise. Lane had just spoken with their attorney and was told that enough time had passed, and they probably weren't going to press charges. Then they got another phone call confirming what I'd been told. I assured her that I was on their side and that this was not what I wanted.

All this time my prayer life was getting stronger and stronger. Prayer was how I coped with the sadness of losing Austin. Not only that but the blanket of God's grace had not lifted from me. He continued to minister to my grief, bringing me constant peace. I had the comfort of knowing where Austin is, and Heaven became more real to me than ever before. I've always had faith in God. I knew that because I had accepted Jesus as my Savior, I would also live in Heaven someday for all of eternity.

I think of it like this, I have a nephew that moved to Australia a few years ago. He is far away. It would take a long time to get there. I know Australia is a real place. That is how I see Austin in Heaven. He simply moved, and when I'm ready to retire, I'm going to move there, too, and see him again.

This is the hope that we have in Jesus, God's Son, created to be born of flesh with the intention of preparing a way back to Him. The story of Jesus is the most beautiful story ever told. He was and is the tangible presence of God on this earth for all to see, for all to choose, and all to be set free and ultimately healed, whether here on this earth or in Heaven for eternity. That is why he is called our Savior. I know that Austin had chosen Him, and I know where he is now—he is alive in Christ.

I continued to pray daily for Austin's dad and his wife and their family. I know how devastated they were, and I hoped that they could have the kind of peace that I found. I also continued to pray for Chris. I knew that he was walking through the greatest trial of his life. I had watched the two boys grow up together. He and Austin had something that was very rare, a love between brothers that was unconditional. He had watched his younger brother take his last breath and he had reached over and placed his hand upon his heart and felt his last heartbeat. I had been holding Chris up in prayer, and as his mom, I will never stop.

It has been comforting to have been on the receiving end of prayer, too. There have been so many people praying for me. I have felt the prayers. That's what it's all about, praying for others. It can move mountains. Don't underestimate the power of prayer. As you will see throughout the story, prayer mixed with faith and love has a tremendous effect on the circumstances that we face.

Alex and his family, now facing this legal battle, have been a major prayer focus. There is a phrase that I had heard while in prayer and I have spoken it out almost daily, *the case against Alex is so full of holes that it is going to fall to the ground and be as naught in Jesus name.* They simply didn't seem to have anything solid to hold up their case.

Hannah was also my major prayer focus. She had lost her brother the Saturday before the last day of school in the fifth grade. She had a very difficult summer, and she had a hard time keeping her emotions in check. Although she was very good about talking out her feelings. We needed her to be in a safe environment.

One day while listening to the radio while at work, I heard an advertisement for a school. Since I was having a slow day at work, I decided to go check it out. God just began to open door after door after door for her to go to an amazing private Christian school close to our home, and two blocks from my work.

It had been about five weeks since the accident, and as I walked through the front doors of the school, I felt the presence of the Holy Spirit. Walking through the tour of the school with the administrator and another parent, we entered the media room and that's when I really felt it! The Holy Spirit was rolling like waves through me! Wow! I thought! God is going to do something amazing through the media at this school!

After the tour I sat and talked with the administrator. He told me a story of a retired couple that would walk around the neighborhood and pray. Every day they would walk right up to the school and lay hands on it and pray for the school to open back up and for it to be a Christian school. I had heard the story before through one of my clients. She lived down the street. She and her husband had been in ministry for years and had planted many churches. I asked the administrator if I could pray for him and he said yes, then I returned to work. There was a message on the answering machine. You guessed it. It was that very client wanting to make an appointment for a haircut! Another confirmation!

Hannah was looking forward to attending this school and even offered to pay the application fee of $100 with money she had saved from a consignment event the year before.

Hannah had already met some of the staff from the school when she had gone to the school-sponsored surf camp that summer. Although she was not fully engaged, she went anyway. She even received the trophy for most improved surfer at the awards ceremony at the camp's completion! (Even though she couldn't stand up and hold her balance on the surfboard).

Right after surf camp she was invited to spend the weekend with some friends at a youth retreat, someone had secretly paid her fee. I was thankful and glad that we could keep her busy. When we arrived at the church to drop Hannah and her cousin Maddie off, I was surprised to see that they had borrowed some surfboards from the very surf camp and school Hannah had applied to.

I knew quite a few of the people going to the weekend retreat. We had all gone to church together where the funeral service was held, and we served in the children's ministry together. I had noticed a couple of the men earlier that week at the new school doing lawn maintenance. There were a lot of these divine connections along the way with prayer and fasting. God's provision blew me away as doors just seemed to fly open.

We were so thankful when Hannah was accepted to the school. It was unbelievable. We used the money that was in Austin's savings account as a down payment for her tuition, and we applied for scholarships. They blessed us with a scholarship, a large portion of the tuition paid by the school. All of that along with some help from her grandparents and Chris and she was enrolled. Everything seemed to fit together perfectly, again like pieces of a puzzle.

The love and care that her new school had shown to her and our family were amazing and helped her heal tremendously. She met a lot of wonderful new friends and mentors. This school, without a doubt, rescued my daughter that year and kept her in a safe environment where she was able to begin to heal. I am beyond grateful!

Hannah had also been enjoying her new-found friendship with her brothers' dad, although it was short-lived. She was ten years old and felt that he needed her in his life because he lost Austin and she thought she could help him by letting him see the Austin in her. Her sense of humor and fun-loving personality mirrored Austin quite a bit.

God also has led me to "a secret place" to go for fellowship and to worship with other believers. It's a place for intercession and prayer, where strong brothers and sisters in Christ (full of compassion) have held me up and kept me from falling apart. Most that come are Christian ministry leaders that can be refreshed and be filled up so that they can then pour out to others.

"The Door" is what it's called. I started attending about eight months before losing Austin. Wow! How it had prepared me (body, soul, and spirit) for this fiery trial. The people there have sat by my side and prayed for me while I just wept. They covered me in prayer, while we praised and worshipped God, the Father, received the love of Jesus, His Son, and were comforted by the Holy Spirit. Praise God for his healing day by day, month by month, year by year. I felt His peace as the burdens released from me, all fear gone. There is healing in the name of Jesus! It has been a process. I felt like it was a time of rest for me, so I took time off from the Healing Rooms ministry, and instead of being in a place to minister I became the one being ministered to. I am grateful for the time I had spent there as well.

Austin had babysat Hannah on Monday nights so that I could go to The Door meetings. The two of them loved their time together. Since the meetings are now moved to Thursday nights, she goes with me often. It's good for her also to be in that environment, and I have seen the healing taking place in her, too. I'm thankful. She has friends around her age that she spends time with upstairs while we are there. They all needed each other, too!

Chapter 8
The Legal Process Begins

So now Alex needed to turn himself in. He had been in California, staying with relatives, trying to heal and find his purpose in life. He was helping at the church where his family attended, doing volunteer work, leading worship for the college-aged kids, and was in counseling there.

Now he had to come back home to Florida and turn himself in. He was scared, really scared. The State Attorney didn't make it easy for him to return quickly. There was already a warrant out for his arrest. Once again, he showed courage as he faced head-on what was before him. He couldn't fly or he would be arrested as he checked in for his flight. He had no choice but to board a Greyhound bus that would drive him across the country. For three and a half days he was in the belly of that bus. Sound familiar? Jonah in the belly of the whale—heading back to a town that he didn't want to go to, to turn himself in. Uncertain of his future and exhausted, he made it to his parents' house in Georgia.

He rested there, and in the morning, they rose, called the family together, held hands, and prayed. Then Alex and his dad got into their car and drove to Florida. The first place that they stopped was at my house. It was almost 9:30 p.m. I knew they were physically and mentally exhausted. We talked and prayed together. I gave Alex something that I had received from a friend the day of the funeral, a silver ring that I had kept on my thumb. It said, *No Fear*. I was wearing it while we were praying, and I felt led to give it to him so he would remember that God was with him and not to have any fear.

> For God hath not given us the spirit of fear; but of power, and of love, and of a sound mind. 2 Timothy 1:7 (KJV)

He took it and thanked me, then took off his silver necklace and added the ring to the other charms on it and put the necklace back on. He said he would always keep it with him. Then they headed off to a friend's house to sleep; tomorrow would be a difficult day.

The next morning, I went to pray with Dawn and another friend. We prayed for a couple of hours before I had to excuse myself and headed over to talk with Mac, Alex's defense attorney. I shared my heart with him over the matter and that this was certainly not what Austin would have wanted, and that I would do whatever I could to help. I agreed with the fact that this was a tragic accident and not criminal.

As Alex had turned himself in that next morning, Mary and Dawn had come over to my house to meet with a detective who had worked for many years in law enforcement and now worked with Alex's defense attorney. He had been gathering the facts of the case and was seeking the truth as we were. He was helpful and transparent and gave us insight into the investigative end of the case. We shared with him what we knew.

After our meeting with the detective, we headed to the courthouse and met with Mac and Lane in the courtyard. I was glad that Mary's best friend Collette had arrived to support her. As she approaches our group, we were all surprised to learn that she and Mac, Dawn and our other friend Toni, whom we had been praying with earlier, had all been good friends throughout middle and high school. For some reason, I think this just got a little more personal. God is working all things together for the good. Once again, we see clearly that He is in the details of our past present and our future.

The bail hearing took place quickly. As we walked down the hall, I saw Austin's dad's family. They looked at me as if I were their enemy. I asked for a hug anyway; they did, but it was very cold.

They didn't walk in my shoes or know the depth of my understanding that God was leading my every step and preparing my mercy motivated heart which led me to respond in a way they had not experienced. They didn't understand the power of forgiveness.

We all went in when they opened the doors. We sat to the right side of the room with Lane, Alex's father, seated between Dawn and me. Alex was visibly emotional, as we all were, but not as much as Austin's dad and his family. They wouldn't allow us to share the whole truth with them as we knew it. Their hearts were closed and guarded, and I completely understood, they had every right to choose to respond that way. This was a turn of events that had ripped open a healing wound and we were all caught off guard. They believed everything that the State Attorney told them on the phone and declined the opportunity to talk to Mac's detective. Had they met with him; he would have answered all their questions as truthfully as he had answered mine. Then they would have had a good balance of all the facts at that point.

They sat over to the left of the room, looking angrily toward us. Austin's dad seemed very broken and emotional. I was fervently praying for him. It was disappointing to see his reaction toward me, since we had all begun to restore our friendship after all those years. I wanted to help them find the peace that passes all understanding. It was as if they had been abruptly turned against us and we had all become their enemy.

I watched as my sister approached the family only to be rejected, and she came back and sat behind me with her friend, trying to understand what had just happened.

The photographer in the corner was a friend from the local newspapers where Dan had worked for many years. She took the pictures that ended up in the paper the next day reflecting our divided view on the charges.

Mac was asked to go first as Alex was at the jail facility in his orange uniform behind the TV screen for all to see as he stood there with courage once again. Mac had told the judge that his client was not a flight risk as he had traveled by bus and car for four and a half days to turn himself in and that he knew where he was every minute. He shared about where the young man had been and what he had been doing there. He shared that he had been a pallbearer at Austin's funeral and had never run away from the charges. He asked that bail be set at $25,000, but the State Attorney said that due to the severity of the crime, his bail should be set at $500,000.

The judge asked if I wanted to speak and I went forward. I was so nervous and didn't have anything planned to say. I walked up there with my heart beating a mile a minute and began to just speak what came to my mind, trusting God to fill my mouth and guide my words.

I said that Alex and Austin were best friends and they loved each other like brothers, and that I knew he would never hurt anyone on purpose. I was so nervous and at a loss for words and said I'm sorry to the judge, that I just was not used to speaking like this. He said to take my time. I took a deep breath and said, "He's a great kid. He's just a great kid."

That was it, all I knew to say at that moment. I sat down. The judge set bail at $25,000 as requested. Just then the representative from the State Attorney's office spoke up and said she had heard Austin's father behind her complaining that if I got to speak, he should be able to speak as well.

He was invited to come up before the judge and speak. Alex was on the monitor screen and I watched his sorrow at his approach. He put his head down and could barely stand the presence of his friend's broken-hearted father. I could tell he was crushed at Austin's dad's outburst in the courtroom. I was earnestly praying for him along with others affected by this sorrowful time. As my ex-husband finished voicing his opinions and took his seat, the judge continued with his earlier ruling of the $25,000 bond, and we were free to go.

That evening around 10:00 p.m. Alex called me from jail to thank me for being there for him. He told me how bad he felt for Austin's dad and for what he had put him through, and that when he had gone back to his quiet cell, he just prayed for him the whole time and hoped that he would be okay. He is such a great kid who has a long hard road ahead of him. I told him that he needed to hug his own dad now and tell him that he loved him. I made him promise and he said, "Okay, I promise I will."

Chapter 9

Trusting God
in Desert Places

I PICKED UP A couple of local newspapers the next morning and each one was written from a different perspective. While one actually had a very factual decent article, the other (the publisher my husband had worked at for 29 years) had a different spin on the story. They left a lot open for interpretation and they built the story up to cause strife and leave the readers with misconceptions, taking a quote that I had made at the bail hearing and printing only half of it. It said that I had stated,

"Austin and Alex were best friends and loved each other." They had left out the rest of my statement, "like brothers." I don't know what they hoped might come out of that, but I didn't appreciate them misquoting me. I felt like I had been used as a pawn in someone else's agenda.

It also happened to be my birthday and I asked Dan for one gift—to cancel his 34-year-old subscription to that newspaper. That was the best birthday gift, to this day, not having piles upon piles of newspapers in my house to constantly clean up on every table, floor, or piled throughout the garage. That's not to mention the articles and stories that carry with them so much negativity, stress, fear and anxiety to a person's wellbeing. If there was ever a good time to fast from the media, it was now.

Turning 47 only two months after losing my son, walking in God's grace every day—you kind of find yourself in a brain fog. I couldn't remember anything. I lived in each moment and made the best of each day. When waves of emotion came, I faced them head on, and moved forward never knowing when they would come or how they will manifest.

Chris just text me a birthday message and a video of the car dealership commercial that he was in. You never know what he is going to do next! He never ceases to amaze me! It's so hard to see him moving forward without Austin, they were so connected. I don't think he really knew how much he loved his brother until he was gone. It was just so evident in the post that he made on Facebook and the interviews on the news and articles from the newspaper. It breaks my heart to see the pain, sorrow and regret in his eyes after our loss.

I was heading out to my birthday breakfast when out of nowhere a strong release of tears just poured forth. Then after my good deep cry, they just dried up, and I was okay again. I remember thinking *where did that come from?* It's God's way of allowing us to mourn and release our deep pain. You know, he catches every tear in a vial. He holds every tear we shed.

"You keep track of all my sorrows, you have collected all my tears in your bottle, you have recorded each one in your book." Psalm 56:8 (NLT)

It was a real gift that Mary and Cousin Nancy took me out for my birthday breakfast. As we ate, we looked out over the Gulf waters. There was a beautiful rainbow, and we talked about God's promise, a sign from Him. The rain began to fall, and I thought about all the tears that I had shed and how perfect walking in the rain would be right now. No one would ever know that I was crying, and I could hide it from the world. Yet God would know. He would catch each tear, separate them from the rain and collect them and place them in a bottle marked *me* amidst the loud thunder and bright lightning, oh the power and awe of our Father God. He is constantly putting things into Heavenly perspective for me and seeing things through His lens has been my guide throughout all of the circumstances.

I love it when it rains. I feel like God is refreshing and cleansing the earth. I can sit for hours and rest in my chair and watch it rain! As I again called to talk with Katrina, God brought us both peace and encouragement in our trying circumstances. We absolutely need to connect to feel grounded and at peace. I have noticed as time goes by and we haven't talked or prayed together, we both begin to feel anxiety.

She told me that Alex was on his way back to stay with his Uncle, as the judge gave him permission not only to leave Florida, but to go to Georgia where his parents live, or to California, where his uncle, his mentor, and his family live.

I am reminded that last year Alex and his cousin took a road trip over the summer and they traveled across the U.S. That must have been divine preparation for this journey alone with God. I pray God will speak to his heart and that he will hear God's voice more clearly than he ever has before.

I am keenly aware of today's date, September 5th, there is a court date today—an arraignment, the first of the court dates and the trial to walk through. I am so grateful that we didn't have to attend. We just continued to pray that God's perfect will would be accomplished: "Romans 8:28-29 (NIV). ²⁸*And we know that in all things God works for the good of those who love him, who have been called according to his purpose. ²⁹For those God foreknew he also predestined to be conformed to the image of his Son, that he might be firstborn among many brothers and sisters.*" This is my favorite verse.

I continued my conversation with Katrina, she told me that Alex's car had broken down just as he had entered California. He was in the middle of nowhere, a desert place, and his debit card had been frozen and marked as stolen. But God was with him as he and his parents worked together to make sure he was safe, and his car got repaired. It was a time for him to trust God while he was in a lonely, desert place. I pray God continues to speak to him.

Before hanging up with Katrina I told her that last night Hannah and I went to a mother-daughter event at a local church. While there I ran into a friend who works at a local Christian radio station. Michelle and her husband also lead a youth ministry and have a group attending a bible college in Redding California in the same town that Alex was going to be. So, I asked if she could have them reach out to him and pray for him since he would be right there in that area. She said to let her know Alex's contact information and she would pass it on to them and gave me a hug.

Chapter 10

Forgiveness and Unforgiveness

I RECEIVED A LETTER from the State Attorney today. My heart beats so fast whenever I see their envelope in the mailbox, I guess from fear of what might be in the letter. This one was informing me of the trial dates that had been set for February.

Once again, I called Katrina and we prayed together, and once again, we put it all in God's hands. As we talked this time, I told her that as orchestrated as this has all played out, I felt I was supposed to write a book when everything is all over! We both felt like it would be a difficult thing to do, but also a real possibility. She said that we just have to have open hearts. It's what we have been living out in our lives, our two families embracing each other and God, trusting Him together while keeping our hearts open and connected, that was the key.

The following Wednesday morning, September 17th. I woke up early at 6:30 a.m. to heavy rain coming down. I sat in my chair on the back porch, lit a couple of candles for light, then I prayed and talked to God and had a good heart-to-heart with Him. I love to watch the rain, smell its fragrance, listen to nature come alive as it brings a refreshing to everything it touches. A much-needed quiet time to sit and rest in its tranquility and peace before waking Hannah.

After taking Hannah to school, Mary called to tell me that she googled and found the police report. I'm not sure I was ready for that, but I had to be. She told me that as she read the facts of the case, nothing seemed to make her angry and she realized that it all pointed to being accidental. I'm glad that she could read it and discern it for me before I had to. She prepared me beforehand. God's grace continued to cover me through what I had read.

As I continued in prayer and trusting in Him to walk us through it all, the number seventeen continues to be a significant number that always seems to get my attention. Kyle text me back and gave me permission to share his phone number with the church group in Redding, I'm sure they would help encourage him.

This story has so many dynamics to it that I'm amazed at the perfect order that God continues to show us through each day. It has been a story of faith, forgiveness, family, friendships, relationships, guns, video games, independence, courage, responsibility, God's grace, love, mercy, restoration, and provision. There are so many words to describe what we have been walking through. These are the positive aspects that we have been focusing on because our mindset is on Christ.

It may sound funny, but I have felt that this story would someday become a movie. Everything that happens has such precise order to it that it would play out as if it were a well written movie script!

There is the other side of the coin for those that don't have the understanding that I have. They may not be looking through the lens of the word of God or standing on God's promises. For some, unfortunately there is unforgiveness, bitterness, anger, sorrow, rejection, their lens from a different, worldly point of view.

Taking on a victim mentality can be a very easy thing to fall into when you walk through any tragedy. I have discovered that a person can become paralyzed in a traumatic memory and not be able to get past it. I know from experience that it can be a vulnerable place to be for one's wellbeing and healing. If you pitch a tent and camp out there, so to speak, for any length of time. It can be debilitating and eventually cause sickness to come upon you. Forgiveness is the key that will unlock you from that prison and brings healing and freedom to every person. I've lived it and I have seen the effects of both.

We are called to forgive so that our Father in Heaven can forgive us. We were not created to carry the burdens of this world; Jesus was. He carried them all to the cross for us. To set us free. Through Him we are forgiven, and because of Jesus doing that for us, "we are commanded to love God with all our heart, soul, mind, and strength, and to love our neighbor as ourselves." It's all about His love. "We are called to love and be loved; against love there is no law" (Galatians 5:23).

When we become born-again believers in Christ, we begin to mature with the fruit of the Spirit, love, joy, peace, patience, kindness, goodness, faithfulness, gentleness and self-control; against such things there is no law. I have found, walking through this difficult time, the fruit that has matured in a person will be what is evident in their life and reactions to the circumstances they find themselves facing.

All the while life seems to be moving on and I must continue to work to pay my bills. It has been a very slow summer at the salon where I work. As each client that comes in either knows what happened already, or asks me how my family is doing, I have found that I am the one to reassure them that everything is okay, that I know where Austin is, and I will see him again, as God's grace continues to cover me.

I had a walk-in client today, referred to me by the business next door. It was perfect timing since I didn't have anyone on my book for the remainder of the day. As he sat down, I asked him what he did for a living. To my surprise, he told me that he worked for the same newspaper that Dan had worked for. I had been avoiding the media, not wanting to give them anything they could use in covering this trial, or twist in any way or to cause strife or disagreement among friends and family members. Well, that was my opportunity to share my heart under my own terms!

I then began to tell him my Austin's story, that I had lost him three months earlier, and that my family, husband, and I were very disappointed in the way his newspaper had handled the story. I told him that my quotes were not complete and led the reader to interpret aspects that were untrue, misleading, and provoking. I began to give him a scenario. I said, "What if you did something wrong and you asked God to forgive you? Would He?"

He said, "Yes."

I said, "Okay. So, what if three months later He comes to you and says, "Hey, you know that thing I forgave you for? Yeah, I changed my mind, and I'm going to *un-forgive* you."

He said, "No, He wouldn't do that. When God forgives, that's it. He doesn't go back on His word."

Then I said, "Neither do I. When I saw Alex at the accident scene I said, 'I forgive you. Austin would forgive you, and you need to forgive yourself. I love you.'"

The man said he couldn't believe it! I said, "I can't *un-forgive* him and I don't want to. I will stand by him through it all and encourage him. It's not my wish for him to have these charges. I am a Christian and it's in my heart to love and forgive." I also told him what it says in the Bible, that if you judge someone you will be judged in the same measure.

He said, "Maybe you should talk to the editor."

I said, "I don't want to talk to the media until all of this is over. I don't want to hinder anything."

As I was finishing his haircut, he said, "You're going to make me cry!"

"Nah," I said.

He told me, "I've learned more from you about forgiveness in 15 minutes then anything I have heard in the last 10 years!"

Wow! I guess that was because God was in the conversation. That's how the Holy Spirit can work through you and direct your words in a manner that will teach the truth. He took my card and before he left, I said, "If you read anything in the future about my son and his friend you will know that I stand with a mercy motivated heart and my son had that same heart. He would say no to the charges, so I say no, too. Now you know where I stand, and you will know the real truth." (Who knows, maybe God will use this divine appointment to honor my wishes).

The following day Dan's brother and his wife were here for the weekend and attended church with us. I had an opportunity to show them the mural of Noah's Ark that I had painted on the nursery wall. It only took us three months to paint it with the help of the pastor's wife.

As we painted and talked, we discovered a work connection between her sister and Chris. What are the chances of that? I think it was God showing me that He was in all the details of my life. He knew everything and He works all things together as you will see toward the end of this book.

Chapter 11

Parallel Story

CHRIS JUST CALLED TO let me know that John, one of his salesmen that worked for him in Tallahassee, had passed away yesterday. It was due to complications he suffered from a year after he had been shot. The irony is that all throughout his story there seems to be a strong connection with ours. Let me begin with sharing a short series of events that led to this point.

Chris had invited Austin to come live with him and work for him. So, after graduating from high school, Austin packed up and made the move. They enjoyed each other's company. They had their ups and downs like brothers do. As I mentioned earlier, Chris fired Austin a couple of times (once on my birthday) and rehired him. Austin couldn't fit into the car salesman roll. He was too honest, too nice, and just not very aggressive or motivated.

After about a year of that arrangement, Chris had a job offer that he couldn't refuse, making a lot of money selling cars in Long Island, New York. He was motivated and excited about the change, but he couldn't take his brother with him, or his two Lab dogs, Max and Ruby! So, his work crew went out to celebrate and say goodbye to Chris. The salesmen and the managers that he worked with headed home as Chris left to drive Austin home to Mom's house!

After celebrating, Mike who was taking Chris' management position, had gotten up in the middle of the night and fallen over a pet gate at the top of the stairs. He tumbled down the stairs and broke his neck. While Chris pulled up to drop off Austin, he asked me to pray for his friend, which I did. I also asked the Healing Rooms to pray and agree with me for his complete healing.

Off to New York Chris went! He had his life packed into his car and no arrangements made yet for lodging! I quickly made a few phone calls and arranged for him to stay at NYSUM Ministry in Long Island City. (He had never been to New York City before and didn't know what he was getting himself into!) However, after a few weeks, things were not going as he had hoped and headed back to Florida. His old job at the car dealership was no longer an option, so his old boss sent him to manage another one of his smaller dealerships in one of the most oppressed towns in the state about 300 miles away! Chris took the job, I later found out this is where my pastor's wife's sister also works.

Meanwhile, Mike who had fallen and broken his neck had recovered. His neck had healed, and he went back to work. Mike and John were working together on the morning of Feb 5, 2014, when a long-time disgruntled employee drove his truck through the showroom window and began shooting with a 12-gauge shotgun. He shot both

John and Mike numerous times while other employees scattered and took cover.

Just at the right time, there happened to be a deputy there getting an oil change for his patrol car. He was standing just down the hall when he heard the gun fire, he quickly charged at the shooter and shot and killed him, but not before taking a bullet himself. The report the shooter had a box of ammunition and some loose shells with him and there was a second fully loaded pump-action shotgun and a .22 rifle fully loaded with additional ammo in his truck. They felt confident that he intended to shoot and kill as many people as possible. The deputy saved countless lives that day by being at the right place at the right time. The deputy was cleared of any wrong-doing and was hailed as a hero after spending almost a month in the hospital healing from his wounds.

Chris talked to me about all of this. "Mom, that could have been me." It was ironic that John had just died from complications of the shooting that had happened a year ago. This had all taken place just three months before Austin was shot.

So, there you have an unbelievable turn of events. I believe that Chris would have been in danger of losing his life at that time, so God routed him to New York through an opportunity He knew Chris wouldn't refuse. I don't know what Chris is going to do or be in the future, but I know that God will use him in a very profound way. Mothers just feel these things. A mother's love for her children is unlike any other love in existence, so unconditional, forgiving, with a true desire for them to succeed in life. We want to see them soar to great heights and accomplish greater things than we would have ever dreamed. I imagine that's the way God sees us.

Chapter 12

God's Perfect Timeline

MONDAY MORNING AGAIN. IT'S wonderful to wake up to peals of thunder and flashes of lightning! Oh, the power of the living God displayed as I sit on my porch sipping my morning coffee. I look forward to going to The Door meeting tonight where there is true freedom to worship! I'm in expectation to meet with the Lord during this set time of prayer and ministry. Truly healing for my body, soul, and spirit. I don't know how people make it through the trials of this life without God, without a Savior, without the constant presence of the Holy Spirit.

On my way I planned on stopping by a local ministry, with Alex's permission, to share his phone number with Michelle, the ministry leader that I had recently spoken with. I have to say that I am once again amazed at God's perfection. He continues to amaze me. I see His fingerprints on everything that concerns me. The night before, as I wrote the note to leave for her, I looked up Alex's phone number in my contacts. As I began to write it down, I couldn't believe my eyes. His phone number was my complete birthday! Wow! That's God saying I know everything that has happened in your life—past, present, and future. It was my day, month and birth year with the Jewish New Year in the middle of the month and year! In three days, however, was the Jewish New Year and the number would be changing from 57"74" to 75. His phone number (which has been changed since) also related to the Scripture verse that I have been standing on (Romans 8:28-29) as well.

> "We know that in all things God works together for the good of those who love him and have been called according to his purpose for those God foreknew he also predestined to be conformed to the likeness of his son, that he might be the firstborn among many brothers."

Alex's phone number was not a coincidence but chosen for him for such a time as this. God knew that I would see it as a sign from Him, that I needed to understand that He was sovereign and in complete control. So, what did I do when I realized this? I sat back in my chair and I prayed, *God, what are You trying to show me here? This is what I heard loud and clear as I listened and waited "It is my timeline"* Wow!

Yes, there is a greater purpose in the details, and I needed to continue to trust God through them (This happened during Rosh Hashanah).

"For your ways are in full view of the Lord and He examines all your paths." Proverbs 5:21 (NIV)

Ironically, Katrina also has the exact same phone number except the year is one digit off, and yes, you guessed it, her birth year!

I had gathered our old home movies and had them all converted to DVDs, maybe one day I will be able to share Austin's and Chris's childhood memories with their dad and his family. They were quickly ready to be picked up and I couldn't wait to watch them all!

Watching our family memories has brought us great joy. I'm praying that one day they will also bring joy to everyone of Austin's loved ones. All we need are open hearts, healed hearts, and willing hearts to move together in unity and peace. In time I believe it will happen.

Ice cream—yes, it's one of those days when God put that feeling of release deep down within me and I knew it was just a matter of time before I would allow it to surface, so I quickly made a plan. I drove straight to Sweet Berries and got a large container of Coconut Almond Concrete and a couple of spoons. I held it together long enough to drive to Dawn's house while thinking about how brilliant my brother was to leave me $50 in Sweet Berries gift certificates for these moments when only ice cream will fix everything!

As my friend opened her door and welcomed me in, I could barely keep it in. As soon as we sat on her back porch and I took the lid off the tasty treat, I lost it! The tears just came up and out of me. I couldn't even talk, so I just cried and ate ice cream because we all know that ice cream makes everyone feel better. Right? She did what every best friend would do. She picked up the other spoon, took a bite and hugged me. And as she began to pray for me, I felt the love of God and the comfort of a good friend. Her just being there with me helped. I didn't feel alone. She just let me cry, and I did, until the ice cream looked like soup in front of me.

After that, I was okay. I had been experiencing these emotional releases in waves from deep down within me, and I realized how important it was to allow them to come up and out. I just felt God's peace flood me—His rest. We all need to learn how to enter His rest.

Last night I went to The Door meeting. There was a sweet presence of the Lord as we all entered into worship of Father God. I have met so many beautiful people at this meeting that I call my Door family and I'm positive that God led me there to draw closer to Him, for healing, and for fellowship. I was surrounded by this family with such love, faith and depth in the knowledge and understanding of God's Word. These are people who love God with all their hearts and who have a Romans 12 mentality.

The prayers of the saints of God, His church, are powerful! Once again, I felt a deep stirring, and I got down on my knees and began to weep. There it was, another wave of emotion being released up and out of me. My friends surrounded me and prayed for me until the feeling of grief passed.

This is such an important step of healing. You must let it all out, or you may not be able to heal properly. If you keep your feelings locked up, like I said earlier, it can bring physical and emotional sickness upon you. That's why you need to let it out and release it from your innermost being. That night I received edifying and encouraging words that built me up in my spirit, soul, and body. I truly felt God's love.

I had a large silk painting with me that I had made into a worship flag. I had created it just before we lost Austin. It was a painting of the ancient open Doors of Heaven looking into the beauty of eternity. It had new meaning to me now that Austin was on the other side of the open door. I felt such freedom in my heart as I waved the flag during worship.

When I arrived home from the meeting, I laid it over "Austin's table," the table I had set up to honor my son. The silk painting covered the table as a prayer covering over the circumstances. On this table I had everything placed that we had received since our loss. Over 100 sympathy cards, countless scriptures, mementos from his friends, a large stack of newspaper articles, a stack of letters from the State Attorney's Office, a football jersey he wore when he played, guitar picks that were left over from his funeral service, a large stack of unfinished thank you cards that never seem to get mailed out. Pictures of his dad and stepmom and their family were there as a reminder to pray for them daily. Even the letter from the Billy Graham Ministries was there.

I had sent a letter to Billy Graham asking for prayer for Alex and our families regarding the tragedy and the legal aftermath. I also explained the forgiveness that my family felt toward my son's friend. I thought if we could have Mr. Graham's prayers, we would find favor with God. It couldn't hurt to try. One of my clients has had a lifelong relationship with him and I had asked a favor of her, to deliver my letter into his hands. However, the letter I had received back from his personal assistant stated he was in the end stages of his life at 97 years old and he was no longer taking personal prayer requests. At least I had tried.

I thought, *what if Alex is called to be one of the next Billy Grahams of his generation?* We must look at the next generation like this. We must have faith in our children, in their friends to encourage them to be who God has created them to be. When I look at this young man, that's what I see, the foundation of a man with a powerful testimony, a broken heart, and a humble spirit. I know that's a pliable man in God's hands. I have also known that if I ever gave up on him that he would give up on himself.

As I have been quieting myself to hear God's voice, I have found that I have no desire to watch TV. I'm pretty sure God's way of walking me through the healing process was to guard and protect my mind, heart and emotions from outside influences. The news, the confusion, lies, and just pure evil that can enter your ears, eyes, and mind, stays there. I just couldn't watch anything other than The Food Network, HGTV, or positive Christian based media channels (stress-free TV). I found I could only listen to positive stories that edified my soul, or I just had to get up and walk away. Quiet time became very important. Keeping my mind fixed on the things of God was essential to my healing process. Having the mind of Christ means protecting what goes in constantly.

Chapter 13

Journal Entries along the Way

HANNAH AND I WENT to volunteer at the street fair tonight. We were helping our church do face painting for children. I have been an artist for many years, and I was trying to figure out why it was so difficult for me to stencil on or even free-hand face painting. My arms felt like over-cooked spaghetti noodles! It was as if my creativity had left my body.

God, what's going on here? I quickly had an understanding to what I was asking Him. I felt like He was showing me that creativity is connected to emotions, and that He had temporarily unplugged my emotions so that I wouldn't be overwhelmed. And in time He would plug them back in slowly when I begin to walk out my healing, and my creativity will return.

Well, that made such sense to me. It's part of the grieving process. Previously, I had gone with my church and had painted faces that night before I lost Austin. That connection may have been on my mind as well. I know that I will be creative again!

Next Thursday night at The Door we will have a special guest, Georgian, a minister from Bulgaria. He and his wife have a ministry there to feed the poor, clothe and shelter orphan children, and dig wells for healthy water. When his mother had been at the Door meetings a few months ago, I had painted/dyed a beautiful stained-glass cross on a lovely silk scarf and given it to her for her birthday. My friend Cheryl had baked a beautiful birthday cake for her as it also marked the one-year anniversary of these weekly meetings, too.

It's been four months since we lost Austin. I've been disappointed by the mixed emotions that his other side of the family have begun to reveal, even Chris. I brought it up today at work when I was cutting Chuck's hair. "Ah, the spirit of cooperation" he stated! As a funeral director he had seen it so many times over the years. When there is a loss God brings restoration during the most important times such as a funeral, but mostly it can be short-lived. Before long people go back to their old mindsets and pick up their offenses once again. That makes perfect sense to me now and I watched as the spirit of cooperation departed.

It's Saturday. I'm always looking for an opportunity for worship time with the Lord. So, Hannah and I went to church for a night of corporate worship. Worship teams from all around the city came together in unity. It was nice to see so many people that I knew.

As I looked over to my right, I recognized a familiar face. She and I had met in New York City at LaGuardia Airport of all places, three weeks before Austin passed. Jennifer and I had gone to minister at NYSUM that weekend and we were heading home. It was our second ministry trip there. The first trip had taken place three years prior; we were blessed with the opportunity to attend Time Square Church with NYSUM on the very day after David Wilkerson's funeral and Oh, how powerful it was.

Our plane was heading to the runway when something went wrong with the controls. We had to taxi back to a gate and get off the plane for an hour while we waited for another plane. As we sat there waiting, we met her and her husband. They said they were from our city and attended this very church. What a small world we live in!

The following Monday night I went to hear a powerful speaker from the Dominican Republic. After he shared his testimony, he called for those that would like prayer to come up. I was drawn to come up and I stood in line awaiting my opportunity. As he prayed for me, this is what he said: *"God's ways are not our ways. Unless a seed dies and falls into the ground, there can be no harvest."* He went on to say that my ministry will be much more powerful after I go through my trial than it had been before. He added that I will have a powerful testimony. *"The enemy has tried to hinder your ministry, but he cannot stop it. Your healing will be accelerated."*

That was such an amazing word! I received it in my spirit because it witnessed with me as truth; yes, my healing was accelerated! You always must remember that if someone "Speaks a word of knowledge or prophecy over you and it doesn't witness with your spirit or edify and build you up" you don't have to receive it, so always be cautious.

Georgian was at the Door again, along with about 70 people, it was a lot of fun! I glanced at my phone and noticed that I missed a phone call from my sister Mary, so I stepped outside and called her back. She was excited to tell me that she had ran into Jared at dinner and they sat and talked for about an hour. He shared with her that he visits Austin's grave often and talks to him there. I believe that was a divine appointment that brought them both healing.

Katrina updated me as to what had been happening in the court case. As she and I spoke she let me know that the investigator said that there didn't seem to be any evidence to back up their weighty claims against Alex. He went on to tell her that he was looking for the truth, as we all were.

God's grace has been sufficient for my family and me. We are making it day by day. We get through each day with God's help. He is the Comforter, and without His help, I wouldn't know how to live or even how to breathe. I am thankful for that. Jesus Christ died on the cross and prepared the way for Austin to enter eternity. I have the hope of seeing him there one day. That gives me peace.

Lane, Alex's dad, sent me a copy of the book he and Alex have been reading. It was recommended by Alex's counselor. It tells about a traveler who was searching for God. It was encouraging to read and connecting with them in this way helped, in the healing process, too.

Chris came home for the weekend and went bike riding with his dad, something Austin used to do quite often, afterwards they went kayaking. I see him trying to fill that void for his father and I think it helps him also. I pray their time together is special for them both.

It's a sacrifice for Chris to come home every weekend for a day and a half. It is a three-and-a-half-hour drive back home every Sunday, after he plays two games of ice hockey with Dan. It was so hard for them to go back out on the ice without Austin's number five. Chris eventually took number five for his jersey to honor his brother; Dan wears the number 7.

As I walk past "Austin's table" I pick up a few sympathy cards and reflect on the love, encouragement, and prayers that have been sent our way. On my way through the house to my quiet place on my back porch, I noticed that I had kind of let my housework go. It's not because I am depressed. It's just that it doesn't seem very important to me right now (ok, probably a little! When you're in depression, you can't clearly recognize it). I just don't have a desire to clean or to cook right now. I'm sure it's part of the healing process, emotionally exhausted. Sooner or later, I'll get my motivation back.

For now, I'll just rest, journal, pray and read God's word for encouragement. I have found such a release when I journal, it gives me permission to forget the things that have been recorded. During prayer I got this picture in my mind of Austin's death becoming a springboard to all of those around him, catapulting his friends into a forced maturity and ultimately finding the importance of their destiny and plan predestined for their life. All of us, family included, have grown in our testimony of how God walked us through each day while strengthening our faith and our love for each other. I felt the presence of the Holy Spirit so strongly as I understood this to be true.

Thursday, October 30. Yesterday I had a very slow day at work. I looked at my cosmetology license and noticed that I had not yet laminated it, so I decided to take it over to Staples, and quickly got it done. As I was pulling into the turning lane to head back to work, I had this feeling I should go over to the gravesite. So, I changed directions and drove over there.

As I pulled up, I noticed immediately that Austin's headstone had been delivered. I grabbed my phone and jumped out of the car, making my way over to it. It was absolutely beautiful. The headstone my son's dad and stepmom found for him was the perfect choice. It was as if it had been made for him and was sitting there waiting for them to find. I was so blown away when I had gone to see it—a guitar stone. I chose a picture of Austin and his beautiful smile for the porcelain picture plate between the dates and had them write along the bottom, *you lit up the world with your smile.* On the back of the stone, with his dad's approval, I had them engrave a design that I drew for it. It was his name and a guitar below it with wings and flames coming out of each side. In the center of the guitar was a door with a cross. It was cool and an honor for me to have drawn it for this purpose.

November 5th. My sister Mary and I decided to visit Chris for the weekend for some much-needed quality time with him and we had a great time. We enjoyed cooking and cleaning for him, but mostly, we just really needed a good excuse to get away. I absolutely love to spend time with Chris. When I'm with him my heart is so full.

When Mary and I headed back home we stopped by the dealership that he managed to drop off his apartment keys. To begin with, it was not the safest area in a very oppressed small town. My sister and I had put anointing oil on our feet before we got out of the car! After all, we had just prayed over his apartment and anointed it with oil, so why not his workplace, too? Moms and aunts will do the weirdest things you know!

In the ten minutes that we were there, he had to deal with a couple of stressful issues. In one case, the wrong vehicle had been transported 700 miles from another dealership, and the customer was there to pick it up. Can you say *stress*? I know God is teaching him valuable lessons that will shape his character as to who God is raising him to be.

We hugged and kissed him then off we went. What a long drive! We decided to stop and stretch our legs at a popular tourist spot, a large dairy farm that had a small country store on the outskirts of our city. We had driven past it on the way to see Chris and we were both feeling curious and adventurous! We picked up some fresh milk and butter and headed back on our way home. My new prayer focus is for Chris to find a new job in a healthier environment!

I stopped by the gravesite today to keep it cleaned up. Someone had put a vase of flowers there on his stone. They were so pretty. I'm glad I'm so close by that I can stop and keep it clean. Austin never let me clean his room, so now I tell him, "Son, I'm cleaning your area and you can't stop me!"

November 10th. Last night I spoke with Katrina again for about two hours. I feel it is so important to keep encouraging her. We need to lift each other up. She said she had been having bad panic attacks and anxiety over the last couple of weeks. She was in Georgia and had taken a job in a popular spa there. However, she wasn't ready to go back to work and she quickly had to resign. It was too much for her. Austin's loss and the insecurity of Alex's future were surely taking a toll on her. So, we prayed together, and that seemed to help. I made her promise that when she was having anxiety or fear she would call me so we could pray together. She promised that she would. We are determined to stick together through all of this.

She then told me that Lane was doing his homework! He was reading his Bible. I told her to have him study about water baptism; I had previously talked to him about it, when he is ready, that would be the next step! She had told me "Not in a thousand years would she have thought he would want to be baptized". Wow! What a privilege that will be!

Chapter 14
Effective Advocate

I KNOW THAT IF God is for us, then nothing can be against us (Romans 8: 31). God is with us and we are overcomers through Him. He is walking through this fiery trial with us. He is writing a story through us. We are a living testimony—a story for all to see, our life being recorded as a family that has hope and forgiveness in our hearts so others may learn from our example.

Nothing surprises God. He knows what we are going to ask for before we ask it. God wants to give us the desires of our heart, after all He's the one who put them there. He wants us to walk in healing, and He wants others to learn how to heal through our example. Don't back down. Don't listen to the lies of the enemy. God will use everything in our circumstances to fulfill His plan for our lives. All we must do is trust and obey Him, even when it doesn't make sense. We will be overcomers and have a powerful testimony if we don't give up. We fix our eyes on Jesus as He died for us all, he made a way where there seems to be no way. He set a perfect example for us, he is our hope, our salvation, and we put our trust in him. Let Austin's life and death bring many into the kingdom of Heaven through his story, his ever-living testimony and through the strength we find in Christ Jesus.

There was good teaching at The Door again last night. The guest ministers (an International evangelist and his wife) were teaching on Jesus and the woman who was caught in the act of adultery. There were men surrounding her, each holding a stone of judgement. Jesus knelt to the ground, took His finger, and drew in the dirt. When He stood up, He said, "Let the one who has never sinned throw the first stone (John 8:1-11). Jesus stooped down again and wrote in the dirt. When her accusers heard this, they threw down their stones and stepped away one by one, beginning with the oldest first. Then Jesus was the only one left with the woman. "Where are your accusers? Didn't even one of them condemn you?" He asked her. "No, Lord," she said. Then Jesus said, "Neither do I. Go and sin no more."

What a good word that was. Just then the evangelist's wife said that she felt there was someone there who felt like there were people *that wanted to gather and stone you.* I knew this was for me because I was upholding Alex and his family. Some people didn't approve and wanted to condemn me alongside of him, and they felt justified in this judgment against me.

She continued, "Because Jesus is with you, they will all throw down their stones and walk away, and it will be over." She added that she and her husband had seen many miracles in their lives then assured me that God has already orchestrated everything and is in complete control, and that it will be fine. Once again, I left this meeting feeling God's healing and restoration.

The next morning, I sat in my quiet place in prayer, feeling God's presence with me. I had been playing soft worship music on Austin's iPod dock. *The Lion of Judah* was filling the atmosphere. As I looked down behind the blue wicker table next to me, past the candles that burn nightly, there was a small newspaper (one that Dan had printed at his workplace) laying on the ground that had been there for a while.

It was folded open to the page that contained an ad for Mac, the attorney that was representing Alex in the case. I realized that I had never read the ad and was led to pick it up and read it. To my surprise it mentioned being an effective advocate rather than casting stones. It said, *"There will always be plenty of people to cast stones at the accused. However, it is my belief that being an effective advocate for the person in this circumstance benefits us all."* That paper had been sitting there for about three months.

I had been praying for an encouraging word last night that would continue to lead me forward. After reading that ad, I knew that it was for me. Yes, everything will be fine, and yes, God had gone before me—before us—and orchestrated these things to all work together for His good, for His purposes. I can't wait to share this with Katrina. I just know that it will bring them all encouragement as it has me. I'd rather be an encourager than a stone thrower any day!

I began to wonder what it would look like if we could all see what God sees, if we could look at people that carry unforgiveness in their hearts like a stone in their hand. A spiritual stone—a rock. Can you see it now? An unforgiveness stone constantly in their hand—how much would that hinder their ability to accomplish simple tasks? People everywhere, your family, at work, at church—how many people would be free to shake your hand without having to put down their stone first?

It's not our place to carry stones. We are called to forgive, to repent, and not judge others regardless of the offenses. Pray that God will reveal to you whether you are a stone carrier, and just drop it once and for all. Repent and don't ever pick it up again. Keep your heart clean and pure and your hands open to receive Gods goodness.

Here is a scripture that I want to share, 1 Peter 3: 11-13 NLT: *Turn Away from evil and do good. Search for peace and maintain it. The eyes of the Lord watch over those who do right, and his ears are open to their prayers, but the Lord turns his face against those who do evil. Now who will want to harm you if you are eager to do good.*

However, stones in the right hands can be a powerful tool for God as well, as in the story of David and Goliath, in 1 Samuel 17– With a stone, David took down a powerful strongman that had been oppressing the people – and keeping them in fear and bondage.

Chapter 15

Mournful Holidays

THE HOLIDAYS ARE QUICKLY approaching—
Thanksgiving, Christmas, and finally New
Year's Eve (Austin's birthday). He would
have been turning 23. I'm not looking forward to any of these holidays, really. We
will notice and feel the empty chair. There
is such a void that we all feel because
someone very special is missing—our joy,
our Austin. Chris was so right when he
said that he was the smile of our family. I
just feel like running away from home until
January, yet I know we'll get through it.

Evidently Chris feels the same way I do about the holidays, so he is headed out of state for a couple of days. I hope he has a good time and gets the rest and peace that he needs.

There were a few surprises to contend with over the Thanksgiving holiday that kept us all distracted from that empty chair, but everything seemed to fall perfectly into place! mM dear client was preparing to head up to North Carolina, where annually, she and her family have had the privilege of decorating Mr. Grahams personal Christmas tree in his private home. I humbly asked if I could send a personal prayer request along with her for the BGM prayer team to intercede for us all. She was happy to oblige. When I shared this with Katrina, she was beyond grateful for the prayer request sent on behalf of her son. Only God could orchestrate these profound things, without His favor, and His blessing throughout the process, I would have given up by now.

It's been six months since we lost Austin, and I'm feeling a bit empty and sad. There's a void of any feeling at all. Now I know what people mean when they say they feel numb. It's like I don't even recognize myself anymore, a bit like dying to self. I'm feeling very much alone even when I'm surrounded by people!

Thank you, Father God, for restoring me to who you want me to be! I yield my life to You, use me as an empty vessel and fill me to overflowing with Your Spirit. Let Your will to be done in my life and in the lives of others and equip me for Your purposes.

I must remember every now and then to stop and yield to Gods plan and hand things over to Him so to speak, if I try to do things in my own power and control, I would totally mess things up!

December 5th—there was a lockdown at Hannah's school today. A tragic event took place in which a man shot and killed his wife and neighbor, then drove to a church and shot and killed the pastor.

She told me that her friends were scared while in lockdown. They were in a classroom and she said to them, "Come on, guys; let's pray." As they started to pray, she said, "Hold on guys. Come out from under the table. You don't pray in fear." So, they all stood and held hands.

She told them that God was in perfect control and that it is all about His plan, and it's not part of His plan for us to die. And even if it was, it's His plan and we need to trust Him. They each took turns praying for the situation and for the families of the victims. She then said, "Okay girls, let's bring it in for a hug." Wow! I can see how the Holy Spirit led her and changed the atmosphere in the room.

Hannah said something interesting today. She said, "It can't end in a tie, Mom, in our situation of accidental shooting versus this man that shot people on purpose. You still have to go to court and see who wins and is free or who loses and goes to jail." That's the perspective of an 11-year-old trying to figure out the difference and the importance of going to trial to break the tie. It remains an unresolved matter until you do.

Chris came home last night for a short visit. I love to spend time with him; I love him so much! He let me know that he would like flying lessons for Christmas! Last August he decided that he wanted to experience the things that Austin had done, so he had gone up on a discovery flight in a Cessna plane. He loved it and decided to go for his pilot's license. My parents, Dan, and I pitched in and bought his lessons for him. When I paid, I put most of it on my debit card but paid part in cash. I felt that the money that was left in Austin's wallet needed to go toward something special, so I paid $71 ("17 backwards") in cash to include Austin in his brother's gift for Christmas.

Christmas came and went quickly and somehow, we all seemed to get through those difficult moments with God's grace. Although I did receive a letter from the State Attorney's office on Christmas Eve, it was for a case management meeting to set a new trial date for the new judge as the original judge was retiring. After all, we had prayed for God to direct the right judge for this trial and for His will to be done. It wasn't what I wanted on my mind on Christmas Day, and kind of took the joy out of Christmas for me.

We decided to take the tree down a couple of days before New Year's, the earliest I have ever put it away. But then again, there were the bare minimal decorations out this year.

I called Katrina to talk, and she told me that they couldn't put up the traditional tree this year. Instead of ornaments, they put little pieces of paper all over the tree. It was a prayer tree. The family spent about an hour at their table writing what they were thankful for, prayers and hopes for the coming year, and decorated their tree with them. After they take down the tree, they will keep the papers in a jar and read them together someday to see how God had answered their prayers and blessed them.

In my weakness I am made strong, even when I feel like falling apart I can't because He is my strength. Today is Austin's 23rd birthday, New Year's Eve! My prayers today are for our family—for my sons' father and stepmom and their family members. It's difficult for us all. I'm praying for them to have peace and healing and for God's love to cover them. I'm praying for Chris today and for God to continue to comfort him. He had wanted to come home and visit Austin's grave, but he had to work.

I know that Alex was probably having a rough day, so I sent him a text to encourage him. He said it was a very difficult day, and he was working on something that he thought I would like. He said he would show me tomorrow when it was finished. I couldn't imagine what it was.

I had called his parents to encourage them as well. Lane said that he had downloaded a Bible app on his phone and was reading the Scripture of the day each morning. Today—Austin's birthday—the Scripture was Hebrews 4:16 NIV. It says, *let us then approach God's throne of grace with confidence, so that we may receive mercy and find his grace to help us in our time of need.* He said that he has already begun to see and feel a change in himself. Praise the Lord!

New Year's Eve, Hannah and I went to the meeting at The Door to usher in the New Year. It was refreshing for my body, soul, and spirit. There is something about putting the past year behind you and starting a new one, especially now. We made it; we got through it.

As I was in the meeting, I noticed that I had a text from Alex. There it was. His surprise was a tattoo on his back, not a small one either. It took up a large portion of his upper left shoulder and back. It was the picture that I had drawn and put on the back of Austin's headstone. It also had a Scripture beneath it of Hebrews 4:16. Yes, the verse of the day on his birthday seemed very fitting for Alex. It helped him get through the day. Now I can honestly say that I am a real tattoo artist!

Katrina sent me a gift in the mail. It was a brass pick that her cousin had brought back from overseas. She sent her two and on them was written *Emmanuel - God with Us*. She knew one was for her and one was for me. It was our promise that God was with us. I put it on my keychain so it can remind me of our unity in prayer and that God is with us as moms going through this difficult time together.

The funny thing is that at church the other day, I looked down on the ground by my seat and there was a silver pick keychain. I picked it up and noticed it had a date on it. As we were dismissed, I walked toward my pastor and a teenager that was standing beside him. I held the keychain up and said, "Do you know who this belongs to? The teenager smiled and said, "That's mine." The date on it represented when he and his girlfriend started to date. God always confirms His words to me through His little signs because He knows I'm always looking for them!

Chapter 16

Answered Prayers

MY FRIEND DAWN AND I made plans to go to a prayer meeting at another friend's house. It was getting dark and I was running a little late. I got into my car and placed my Bible in the back seat. Looking looking both ways for cars I began to back out of my driveway when I felt my cars back tire lift a little. *What was that?*

I knew right away that I had run over one of those ducks that had been sleeping at the end of our driveway. I felt a knot in my stomach as I got out of my car to check. I saw him staggering and falling down. Oh, my goodness! The poor thing was bleeding from his beak. I honestly couldn't handle it. I couldn't deal with watching this wild duck die in front of me, knowing that I was to blame.

I got back into my car and started to drive away and called Dan. I told him what had just happened and that I needed him to call the animal rescue right away. I said, "Whatever you do, don't tell Hannah. I don't want to upset her. Please don't tell the neighbors that I am responsible. They will never talk to me again." Our neighbors loved this duck and had named him Munster and fed him every day.

So, of course, he told Hannah. They found the duck out by the street, and he had blatantly confirmed, "Yep, the duck is dead" right in front of her. Yes, you guessed it Dan called the neighbors over who had named the duck and they both cried over their loss.

I was sick to my stomach. I felt so terrible. I pulled up at Dawn's house and she got into my car. As we drove off, she asked me what was wrong. So, I stopped the car and said, "I killed a duck, an ugly duck, and I feel horrible. I killed it because I was running late for a Bible study! I didn't look at the end of my driveway before I backed up."

I continued to feel worse and worse. When we arrived and went in, we were offered some refreshments. At that moment I didn't have an appetite for anything. While I sipped my iced tea and sat there at the table, I had a little mini vision in my mind, it seemed so real! I started to laugh so hard that I couldn't seem to stop. Dawn and everyone else were looking at me and waiting for an explanation. So, I settled down, and told them what I saw.

There was Austin at his mansion home in Heaven. He stepped out his front door and began to walk down his long sidewalk. Down in front of him was Munster the duck waddling up to him. He stops and says, "Oh, come here, little buddy. Did my mom kill you? It's okay. You can live here with me. I have a lake out back you're going to love!" Then he picked him up and turned around and he walked back into his mansion with his new pet. I was instantly okay!

Early that next morning as I lay in bed, I began to wonder what that was all about. Then God spoke profoundly to my heart, this is what I heard "If that is how you felt over an insignificant wild duck that you were responsible for killing, what measure of pain do you think Alex is going through having taken the life of his friend and your son?" I was just feeling a fraction of what he was going through, but that little insignificant event put it all into perspective for me.

While I was at The Door meeting Chris called me to let me know that he was locking the door for the last time at the dealership where he had been working. I recently felt led to look up stats on that area and was surprised to find that it ranked as #8 in the most dangerous places to live in Florida and #2 in the worst places to live in Florida. I was so relieved and happy for his decision to leave that depressed area.

When I had traveled with him on that horrible 20-mile highway that took him to work and back home every day I realized how utterly dangerous it was. He had applied for a job closer to where he was living. The opportunity opened and he took it. Change is good. He starts on Monday! Truly an answer to prayer! (This is where he met his beautiful bride!)

This morning I went to the courthouse at 8:30 for a trial hearing. I didn't have to be there, but I took the opportunity anyway to speak with the attorney, Mac. I'm glad that I did. After the hearing, we walked down together, and I shared with him the fact that we were praying for him. He thanked me. I took that opportunity to show him the picture of Alex's tattoo and he was amazed by it. It revealed to him how much Alex cared for Austin.

As we stepped outside of the courthouse, I asked him if I could pray for him, and he said sure. I prayed for God to give him supernatural wisdom, knowledge, and understanding, and for an increase of discernment and for truth. I prayed for God to give him favor in his cases and for God to shine His light in the dark places as truth is revealed to him. What a great opportunity to pray outside the courthouse doors! He asked if he could give me a hug and I said sure. Off to work I went contemplating the next court date and the beginning of the trial.

Hannah had been struggling in school from the beginning of the year. Honestly, she was spiraling downward, and I had been working behind the scenes trying to help her keep up with her heavy homework load. We duel-enrolled her in the public-school system and started walking her through the long grueling testing process which took the full school year. Finally completing the process on the last day of school! We are hoping to get an IEP in place to help her navigate through each school year ahead. We are blessed to have the private school behind us every step of the way and I'm convinced as they had been advocating with us has helped the process go more quickly than expected. They were willing to help us in any way they could. Two of her teachers, one being her school mentor, took time away from their school day to attend a meeting as the school board began the process of evaluating her.

I know that the trauma of losing her brother the Saturday before the last day of fifth grade left Hannah with the need for emotional healing and had a lot to do with the challenges that she was now facing. I could tell because I had been suffering the effects of trauma, too. Memory loss, I couldn't process information, lack of motivation, lack of focus—I recognized my own symptoms in her. Now, with testing we were able to pinpoint her weak areas and begin to lead her in the right direction.

We also had an amazing professional advocate help us through each step of the way. If I hadn't had her with us, it would not have gone so smoothly. She interviewed Hannah at her office and had her consultation completed quickly, along with her physician's diagnosis. This answered a lot of the questions we had and provided the support that Hannah needed.

It turned out, as we were learning the truth about Hannah, we stumbled upon something unexpected and "self-diagnosed" Dan with Asperger's! Like fireworks going off in my head, almost every question that I had ever had about his routines and behaviors, social skills, inability to empathize at times, difficulty making eye contact with new people, restricted interests, sarcastic humor to fit in, and difficulty with fine motor skills. Finally, through understanding we have all gained breakthroughs

This was almost too much to handle while we were just recovering from losing Austin and helping Hannah to be successful in school. But then I had remembered that just a few days before when Dawn and I were praying together, we had prayed and asked God to reveal the whole truth to us concerning the struggles that had been hidden in my family. Wow! He had just answered that prayer.

Dan was upset for about a week until he processed the information and came to terms with it. He finally said, "Well, I guess you are right. I'm pretty sure that explains why I sometimes behave the way I do." Then it happened, with each week that passed he really began to grow in areas I never would have imagined!

The good news is that once you have identified something you can now move forward and not be afraid to make some changes, to grow past your fears, routine patterns and strongholds. The amazing part of this new awareness was watching the new growth take place in areas that had been previously frozen and set in a definite unchanging routine. You can try new things, new foods, do things on the spur of the moment, grow socially, do the dishes at Thanksgiving! There were so many more opportunities now for us to all to grow as a family than before we had figured this out. Freedom!

Chris called me today. As always, I was glad to hear his voice. I was surprised to hear him say that he wasn't as mad at Alex as he was a few weeks ago. Amen! I told him that he needs to forgive so that he can continue to heal. I pray for a true revelation for him to forgive completely. He was calling to find out about the new court dates, and I told him what I knew.

I called Katrina to let her know about the meeting I had with Mac and to also let her know that I had shown him Alex's new tattoo. She was glad that I had prayed with Mac, and of course, she and I prayed together on the phone before we hung up.

Chapter 17

Downloads and Revelation

As I WAS IN prayer tonight, I was reminded of when we were in our old church. Austin was about 15 and there was a guest speaker ministering up at the altar where I was getting prayer for something. Austin was out with the youth playing basketball. I saw him come in through the side door. He came up to me and said, "Mom, I jammed my finger with the ball and it really hurts." The guest speaker approached Austin and said, "Young man, there is a call on your life."

As a mother I was so happy to hear those words spoken over my son. I asked the Lord, *was this not true? What was this call that was upon him, upon his life?* As I sat for a while and waited on the Lord, I heard; *Austin's call was in his death.* I didn't just hear it; I felt it as well. I felt God's power flow through me with those words. Then I headed to work thinking about what I had just experienced. I felt there was more to it and continued to wait on the Lord.

The next thought that I heard carried more power through my body and I couldn't deny that it was something to pay attention to. It was revealed to me while I was working on a client. This is what I heard; *Alex is going to be one of the next Billy Grahams that God is raising up for His end time harvest.* Austin had catapulted Alex into his destiny, into his greater calling.

As I began to process what I was hearing and feeling, I realized that the woman who was in my salon chair was a dear lifelong friend of Billy Graham, one of her family members having worked closely with him for many years. Then I remembered what Dan and I had purchased less than an hour before we lost Austin. It was Billy Graham's *My Hope America* DVD that we had planned to watch together.

I don't believe that this was a coincidence, but a revelation of what God wanted to do. I know that I must continue to stand with Alex and walk him through this process. If it is true and Austin's call was in his death, it is my responsibility to make sure that it wasn't in vain. I had to do my part to love and forgive and to be a mom to the youth around me.

As I woke up this morning, I have had so many thoughts buzzing through my mind. I was remembering the last time I had spent with my son, just the two of us.

I had asked him to drive me in his truck to Home Depot to pick up six sheets of foam board for Vacation Bible School projects. They didn't have what I needed there, so we had gone to Lowe's. He was so funny as we walked together arm-in-arm. I love that he was worried that someone would see him there because, as an electrician, he was a Home Depot guy!

He had been silly and goofy, but so respectful to me. He had plans to meet his friends for dinner, and they called him a couple of times while we were out. He assured them that he would meet them as soon as he could, but he was doing something for his mom right then.

As we walked around, he didn't make me feel rushed, and when I asked him if he wanted to hear about the ministry trip that I had just returned from he said, "Tell me, Mom. I want to hear all about it!" He listened to the highlights of my trip and kept saying, "Wow! That's pretty cool, Mom!" He was so genuine toward me and the details of my adventure; it was such an amazing time together. I love that, in our last real conversation, we talked about the Lord and ministry for the women in the New York homeless shelters. We headed back home and soon he was off to meet with his friends.

Recently Chris and a friend drove up for a weekend visit to our house. While Chris had a flying lesson that morning, the rest of us went to church together. The preacher was teaching from Galatians and gave the scenario of a person who had murdered another person. The point was made that this person, though he should expect the worst punishment for what he did, through God's mercy and grace and through His Son dying on the cross, the man could be forgiven.

I leaned over and whispered to my son's friend, "That is why I forgive Alex." She lovingly put her hand on my shoulder. I had my notebook out, and just then, I was prompted to write this down, I believe Chris is going to be a preacher one day! She read it, then took my pen and wrote under that, that was just in my mind!

I'll take that as confirmation! Just this morning Chris had come out from his bedroom singing I'll fly away, oh glory! I'll fly away. When I die, hallelujah, by and by, I'll fly away! I told him that Austin had sung that in his little white cap and gown at pre-school, missing his two front teeth, of course!

While we were on our way to church, I Will Rise came on the radio. I had said that it was one of the songs that we played at the funeral. When we had gone to church, both songs were played during worship! God knows everything!

Chris enjoyed his flying lesson, this time he took off up into the air on his own! He was nervous, but he did it, what a confidence builder! He told me that flying gets easier each time he goes up, I'm so glad that he sets these challenges for himself. Is this the same kid that took off his snowboard at the top of Snowbird mountain and thought he would walk back down because of his fear of the high steep mountain? I'm glad that I made him put it back on and prompted him to face his fears that day! I'm so proud of him.

I got a revelation last night while at a prayer meeting with friends. As we prayed, I began to get a download of this idea about video games! I felt strongly like it was from the Lord. I believe this represents a major gap that needs to be filled.

The last thing Austin had purchased 30 minutes before he died was a video game download. My thought is that kids can become so desensitized to guns because of these games. But what if all these games with guns and weapons in them were to have a gun safety course added as the first level of play? They would have to go through the course to get to the game. It could teach them practical truths about a real gun and the dangers, bringing balance and a healthy fear of guns back to these kids and young adults. This could help them realize there is a genuine difference between a video game controller and a real gun.

I think it's a great idea since so many gun-related deaths are connected to hours and hours of shooting while playing the games. If that were put into place, we could help stop some accidental shooting deaths and save countless lives. I would love to see these video game giants also become proactive in the prevention of gun violence and accidental deaths by donating a portion of their video game proceeds toward victims or family members of shootings that are linked to violent video games to cover funeral expenses and support for grieving families.

At our weekly Door meeting, I had been praying with two other volunteers I know from the Healing Rooms. One of them is our local director and she brought me a powerful prophetic word: *God has gone before you and he has made the bed. He has smoothed it out and removed every wrinkle. He has folded and tucked in the corners tight—a bed made military-style so that you could bounce a quarter off it!* Immediately I thought of the ongoing trial and every aspect of it. Every wrinkle has been removed. Yes! I can have faith to believe that!

So, the next day, as an act of faith, I stripped the bed; cleaned my sheets, blankets, and pillowcases; and remade my bed. I smoothed out and removed every wrinkle I could see. I tucked in the corners tight! What an amazing night's sleep I had. Sleeping on a fresh clean bed has a way of giving you a peaceful night's sleep. That was not all, it was also the fact that I believed that God had everything in such perfect control.

Valentine's Day. As I quietly slipped out to buy Hannah her Valentine's Day surprises, I carefully picked out a card, a heart-shaped box of candies, and some makeup remover wipes. Then I picked up the final gift, her favorite cookies-and-cream candy bar. As I did so, I noticed a larger one, so I switched them and headed for the register.

It was a bittersweet moment as I also remembered showing my love for Austin and Chris at February 14, as I quietly slipped out to. When the cashier rang up the amount of an even $17, I was amazed. It was as if Austin was saying, "I love you, too, Mom." What a great way to start the day! I kept the receipt and put it in my Bible.

As I got to work, I had another surprise. It was an envelope from my client containing the response from the office of Billy Graham Ministries. I waited until my work was finished. After work, I drove to Austin's graveside to read the letter. There was a car parked in front of mine along the road. As I sat on the bench (that my sister and I had bought from Home Depot the week before), I met a woman tending to her son's grave. She said, "Are you his mom?" As I walked over to speak with her, I said yes, and we introduced ourselves to each other.

I have wanted to meet this woman ever since I had noticed the dates on her son's gravestone. They stood out to me, as did how immaculate she kept his grave. Her son had died of a drug overdose.

He was born a year and a week before Chris. She also had her pre-dated stone connected to his and I noticed our birthdates were just days apart and the same year.

She went on to tell me that he was an amazing kid, but he had been caught up and hooked on pills. She said it had been three years, then she broke down and cried. "It's so hard," she said. She was having such a hard time getting past it. I prayed with her and encouraged her to go to the Healing Rooms for more in-depth prayer and gave her their business card. We also exchanged phone numbers. Every so often I come across it in my contacts and say a prayer for her.

Meeting her today was a God-thing. I went back to Austin's bench and finished reading the letter that I had received from Billy Graham Ministries. It was encouraging, but not what I had expected.

As I sat there and spent some time in prayer, I felt God was showing me something about Austin's birthday, New Year's Eve. It was on the last day of the year to represent the last day, the harvest—the end-time harvest. I believe he was reserved for the last days' harvest of souls and his story and testimony will bring many in when it is told. How encouraging to be praying to God and waiting on Him quietly, not trying to think about anything, and have that just pop into your mind. You must wonder, *was that God?* I do believe that it was.

I was at The Door meeting again when I heard this word loud and clear: *petition*. It was around midnight after we had worshipped for a while and were resting in the gentle, still presence of the Lord. I had felt led to share my idea to have as many people as we could to write letters to the State Attorney to show support for Alex. We prayed corporately over the matter. Cara said that she had also been hearing the word *petition* all evening! *Well, I'll have to continue to pray about that,* I thought.

Chris sent me the most amazing text message tonight after I had sent him one for Valentine's Day. I am so blessed to have such an amazing son! He has such a love and respect for me.

The other morning as I was waking up, I heard this amplified: *It will be over before it begins!* This has proven to be the most unpredictable year of my life. The most challenging, most equipping, painful, healing, faith-driven, grace-covering, merciful, Holy-Spirit-leading, forgiving year of my life. I have grown more in understanding, wisdom, and faith at this time than in all my years on earth.

Chapter 18

Overcoming Fear

I AM SO GLAD that Hannah's in a small Christian private school this year. On Mondays the school day ends with a chapel service. They have a student worship team followed by a heartfelt message, and relevant Scripture verses. Each year all the students are assigned a carefully and prayerfully chosen mentor (from coaches and teachers) that they can trust and talk to about anything. They meet weekly in their small group at the end of the day on Fridays.

Having someone to talk to during that difficult time in her life was priceless.

Like many kids her age, Hannah preferred to be with us and would worry at the thought of being left alone in a youth group or similar situation. I couldn't just drop her off at school any earlier than five minutes before the bell rang, she had just enough time to get to her class. Keeping her in a safe environment has become one of the most important things to focus on. Thank God she has pressed through and come to an understanding of what has been holding her back. Through prayer and maturity, she has overcome and moved past most of the things that she had struggled with after the loss of her sibling.

It's about taking authority over each fear and replacing it with the truth. *Who does God say that I am?* Or taking a negative and replacing it with a positive. Where there was anxiety, you can replace it with the substance of peace by getting into God's word. Where there was fear, just step out in faith and be willing to trust and believe that nothing bad is going to happen. The more you practice being in God's presence through worship music and standing on His word, the more peace you will have!

It's also about constantly moving into a healthier routine and then a still healthier one. With time, prayer, and patience we can all learn to overcome and break free from all the unhealthy things that control us. That is the amazing thing with God.

He loves us so much that He reveals the truth to us, and that truth shall set us free No longer will fear hold us back from enjoying the good things in life. You never know when you might be missing out on something that you will love! That's how you overcome and move on. Don't be afraid to try new things.

I'm far from perfect and I have many of my own areas to work on. I need to get back to where I was before I was bumped off course, but I don't know what that looks like anymore. I'm sure it won't resemble my life before all of this happened. After all, we can never go back.

Things will be forever different, some good and some bad, but we will continue to trust God to lead and direct us.

I had a dream last night that Chris had gone through the fiery trials and come through them to the other side and that God was restoring him and healing him. This dream was encouraging for him and for me.

Now Hannah and I were leaving this week's Door meeting. It was late (around midnight), it was a chilly 37 degrees, and one of my friends had gone with us. The sprinklers along the sidewalk were hissing and thinking it was a snake, Hannah got scared, turned around and ran back down the driveway and back into the house. I turned around and went back to get her, but it took me about ten minutes to convince her that it wasn't a snake!

After we drove my friend home and headed toward our house, we approached the entrance to our housing complex. There had been a very bad accident at the entrance. A car had taken out the fire hydrant and there was water shooting up high into the air. Police, fire trucks, and an ambulance had just arrived. I'm guessing it had just happened within the last ten minutes as the fire station was only two blocks away.

Just then Hannah started to cry and said, "I don't know why, Mom, but every time I see an accident since we lost Austin I want to cry." Just then I realized that Hannah's going back into the house for ten minutes may have saved our lives. Or if we had been the first ones to the scene it would have been traumatic for both of us. After I put her to bed she and I prayed for the people in the accident. Right then I heard a medical helicopter flying over the house and I knew it was serious....

Chapter 19

Stand by Me

I'M FEELING SO EMOTIONALLY drained, like a whirlwind is all around us. Hannah's struggle with schoolwork spills out onto me at home. After working all day on my feet, then making dinner, I sit with her about four hours doing homework. It gets to a point where I have nothing left. I'm just done, but then we'll do it all again tomorrow. However, each day God's grace is enough as His strength is made perfect in my weakness. Dan even offered to do the dishes from then on to take some of the heavy load off of me! What a blessing he is.

As I was waking up this morning, I heard Proverbs 3: 5-6 NIV: *Trust in the Lord with all your heart, lean not on your own understanding; in all your ways submit to him and he will make your paths straight.*

Yesterday I took Katrina with me to the Healing Rooms for prayer, we had a blessed time of ministry, then we had lunch together at the Cheesecake Factory and spent some time talking and praying. On our way home we stopped by the Christian bookstore. I wanted to buy Lane a gift—His first Bible. We waited while his name was stamped in gold lettering on the front cover and Katrina took it back to Georgia with her and gave it to him.

I woke up this morning thinking, *If He'll bring you to it, He'll bring you through it.* Then at this week's meeting at The Door it was that time again, time for a good cry. I cried and cried and cried. It's like the emotion and tears are stored up until they need to be released. Then whoosh! Oh, the release that I felt when it was all done. I felt as light as a feather, still covered by God's grace.

The host, Cara, sat down beside me and said, "How are you doing? Are you okay?" I said yes but started crying again. I thought all the tears had come out. I guess I had a few more that had to be released. She then began to give me some amazing compliments. She said that she looked forward to my coming and seeing me every week. She recognized that I am genuine, and I love God and I want to please Him. She said that I'm always thinking of and praying for others. Then she prayed for me to have someone stand by me whenever I need it, that I would always have someone by my side. How sweet that was. I felt so accepted and loved.

The next day at work I realized that Jennifer and I had worked together for more than 20 years—indeed, a good friend standing by me! She had lost her son at 19 years old, and she has played a big role in the process of my healing. Over the years I have listened to her testimony of losing her son and I've watched her minister and pray for women who have lost children. She had gone before me and helped prepare me. She understood everything I was going through. Yes, what a true friend to stand by me!

I'm sitting in my car at the tip of the Island, looking out at the gulf water, praying, reading, writing, and listening as I desire to hear His voice. I'm eager to hear Him tell me exactly what is going on, what He is doing, and what He wants me to do. It's when He is silent that I must just continue to trust Him.

Chapter 20

Mother's Day & Selfless giving

I WENT TO AUSTIN'S grave today to water the flowers and plants. I was feeling tired and so down, I began to pray and cry. I told God that I was tired of trying to figure things out. I was just plain tired. I asked Him what he wanted me to do.

Just then my phone rang. It was the victim advocate I had met at the scene of the accident. She told me they were having their annual vigil for victims of violence soon. She said if I wanted to bring a picture of Austin to put into the collage I could. (I assume that she had called his dad as well.)

As I hung up the phone I began to ask if this was God's answer to my question. Should I go? I had mixed emotions because I didn't really believe in my heart that it was a violent crime. It was a tragic accident, yes. But a violent crime? No. I had to pray about it. I looked up the vigil online and found that I knew the person in charge. I also knew about the tragedy that had touched her family years ago.

I decided to pray about what I should do and let God direct me. Every day I know that God is divinely transforming us, developing our character to be more and more like the image of His Son as we trust and yield to Him. When we sacrifice our flesh daily, we become more like Him. It's not through anything we do, but through the Holy Spirit within us that we are cleansed and purified as we go through the fiery trials of this life.

I went to see Katrina at her spa yesterday and we had another good talk. We also prayed about our situation, and we prayed for Chris and his dad's family, for Alex and for Jared. We talked about possibly being led to do a women's group one day. We always feel so much better after we get together to talk and pray and encourage one another.

I can't help but think that the gun was destined to go off that tragic night and the plan God allowed to unfold He turned toward His greater purposes. He has equipped me to stand in the gap, but I'm so tired!

I decided to attend the vigil and Hannah and I met up with a friend there. When I pulled up, I saw a news van. I knew that I didn't want them to know who I was. As we walked along the River walk, there was a man that was setting up his news camera and saw me taking my daughter's picture. He offered to take a picture of the two of us with my phone. I was glad that he didn't ask me who I was or who I had lost. I'd been trying to steer clear of the media. I decided not to put Austin's picture in the collage of victims as I didn't feel led to do so. I didn't want to see him on the news again. The friend we met there released a dove at the end of the meeting. It was a touching evening.

When it was over, I called Katrina and shared with her some of the details from the evening's events. She was glad that I went. We talked more about creating a women's support group and how we could call it From Broken Hearts to Open Hearts, who knows, maybe one day. But for now, it's filling the void that we feel, and creating a purpose for our pain. We could even have an annual dove release.

I need to say, "I love you, Austin. I miss seeing you. I miss your hug. I love you, my baby boy! You are and always will be amazing."

Chris came home last night and of course, he made Hannah's day when he took her to school in the morning! I love it when he comes home. I believe that God has been doing some major testing in him and his character not only through our recent tragedy, but through his many real-life experiences. He has gone through more tests and trials than any 26-year-old I have ever met. The things that he has encountered in his life could be a bestselling novel—you just can't make this stuff up. I'm sure that he's learned a lot from his own mistakes. I won't be surprised when one day he realizes just how much wisdom and discernment he carries, to help other people to not make the same ones.

It's Mother's Day weekend and it's a tough one but I know I'll get through it. I'm praying for a good weekend. God will walk me through it. After church on Mother's Day my sister in-law, Chris and I went to visit our friend Jackie as it was a very special day. Not only was it Mother's Day, but it would have been her son's birthday. She had told me that after Bryan had lost his battle with ALS at the age of 27 and moved to Heaven, every year something special happens for her on or around his birthday. It was as if he was sending her a special sign, a hug from Heaven!

I knew what God wanted us to do for her. It was our turn this year to fulfill that gift of love for her. Quite simply, we were all tied together inexplicably in a way that made this Mother's Day very special and dear to us.

It just happened that Chris' mom's husband was also grandfather to Bryan. In going through her father's things after his death a few years ago a baseball was found in his desk drawer. It came rolling towards her when the drawer was opened. A sticky note was attached to it indicating that it was a Game Ball from one of Bryans wins! It was time for that ball to get back into his mother's hands, time for her to hold the long-forgotten game ball that he had held.

Jackie's sister Joyce met us outside and we all went in together to surprise our unsuspecting friend. She was happy to see us, and at the same time, completely taken by surprise. A gift bag was handed to her containing the baseball wrapped in tissue paper. It was explained to her where it had come from. Holding it gently, she said that her son loved to play baseball and that he was very good at it. She said, "As a matter of fact, this must have been a game ball after a win that he had given to his grandfather." She began to cry and couldn't find any words to say, but it was the gift she had been waiting for all day. We were all crying with her.

She found a perfect place for the baseball on a table beside her bed. She thanked us for being so thoughtful—that's how we made it through Mother's Day. I was missing Austin. My sister-in-law was missing her mom, who had also recently moved to Heaven. This dear friend was missing her son. To be able to put it all into perspective and bring joy and happy tears to another mom made the day worthwhile.

It's Sunday again, and I really felt led to visit the church where the friend I had met in New York attends. They were having a speaker that I wanted to hear. He had such a powerful testimony. It was nice to see my friend again as I realized that it had been one year to the day since we met in New York with NYSUM Ministries again, God's perfect timing!

When the guest minister mentioned that he felt there were people there who had a book to write, I instantly felt like bursting out into tears. I knew he was talking to me, although I didn't have an ending yet. I still didn't know the outcome, but I knew God was going to walk me through to the end. That was the second time this week I heard that I needed to write a book! So, this was just confirmation.

A friend of mine called to tell me that as she was driving up toward the convention center on her way to work, when she saw there was a gun show. She had already been praying on her way to work and felt led to drive into the parking lot and pray that the guns wouldn't get into the wrong hands or be used for harm. She knew that she needed to take it seriously, so she prayed it through. When she finished praying, she knew that she needed to let me know. I'm grateful for her love and obedience. We all need to do that more—pray when God leads us to pray!

June 2nd. Hannah and I came home from shopping to find that a bouquet of flowers and a beautiful ceramic candle had been delivered by the front door. They were from Kate, Austin's friend. How thoughtful as she has remembered every year since the accident to send me beautiful flowers (she will soon send a heartfelt note with the final and biggest bouquet arriving on the fifth-year anniversary. I have no words to express the gratitude I have felt for this beautiful, compassionate, amazing young woman). The year anniversary was coming up and she wanted to cheer us up. Austin was like a brother to her; she had been answering the 911 dispatch phones the night of the accident and had taken the difficult call. There is so much that God is doing in and through the lives of those who knew and loved him. He has so impacted all whom he knew.

As Hannah, my sister Mary, and I were getting ready to go on a trip to Virginia the water heater in our house went out and flooded the floor in the kitchen. It was time for it to go; it was on its last legs after 24 years of service. Why do things like that happen just as you're leaving town? On a brighter note, it turns out that my sister and I are now starting to attend the same church. That is so exciting for me!

It's Saturday morning in Arlington, Virginia, and it has been an interesting weekend. I'm lucky to be here. I was almost put on the National No Fly list! As we were going through airport security, they detained me while they ran my purse through the X-ray machine and began examining it. I have flown so many times and never had a problem, what could it be? A female cop was called to come and take my purse to the police section and I began to get nervous. She said, "Ma'am, you have two live rounds in your wallet."

What? Oh, my goodness! I couldn't believe it, but it was true. When I had gone to visit Chris, while he was at work, I was cleaning his apartment and noticed he had Austin's gun chest. I had opened it and although his gun had been confiscated, there was his clip and a box of bullets he had purchased the day of the accident. I had decided to take a bullet from his clip and one from the box and when I got home, transfer them to my jewelry box for a keepsake. I had put them in my wallet, but I forgot they were in there! How ironic that it was on the one-year anniversary of Austin's death; Wow! You just can't make this stuff up. I didn't know that my wallet was loaded. I didn't know if I was getting arrested or released to fly!

I finally made it to the gate as they were getting ready to close the door. It had taken a while to explain the situation to the investigators so they could release me to go. Oh my! We were the last ones to get on the plane, but off we went. The reason for our trip was to attend my brother's retirement ceremony after 24 years of service. Andrews Air Force Base in Washington, DC is not a place where you want to have two live rounds in your wallet! The officer did mention that I might get fined up to $500 per bullet. I prayed that I didn't. (I didn't get fined.)

We had an amazing time with my family. It was a good distraction to be with them. Family is so important at times like these. I'm so grateful to mine for respecting my point of view and for coming alongside to support me in the stance of forgiveness I was taking toward Alex. They were sensitive to my feelings and to my faith.

Chris was taking a cruise with his friends as a distraction from the anniversary. However, in true fashion for him, he had his passport at my house in his accumulating pile of mail. Running late and driving toward the Port he got caught up in traffic and didn't have time to run by our house to grab it! Or he would miss the Cruise Ship! He called me and asked how we could get someone to meet him at the interstate exit with his passport! Quickly I had my BFF Dawn find it and meet him on the way to the Port. They met up by the highway exit, she said a prayer over them, and they made it just before they closed the ramp. That's Chris for you—a perfect example of his planning! Happy 27th birthday, Chris! We both were the last ones to board!

Chapter 21

Austin Wouldn't Want This

MY HEAD IS SPINNING with all the things I feel led to do in preparation for the upcoming trial. I wasn't ready emotionally and I didn't feel prepared. Have I done all that I can to help Alex through this difficult time? Have I given enough support to his family? Have I given enough support to Chris? Have I covered him with enough prayer? What is he thinking? How will he testify? Will he be upset with me forever with my stance of forgiveness? Will he ever understand?

This must be the most difficult situation that Chris has ever been placed in, to love both of your parents unconditionally, understand each side, but have your own feelings to contend with as well. There was a plumb line snapped right in the middle and he had to walk it. A perfect balance, his plumb line of love showed great maturity and respect. I just must yield to God's will in every area of my life. Lord, let Your will be done in Jesus' name.

In my heart I feel drawn to write a letter to the State Attorney's Office to officially let them know that I am not in agreement with these charges. I don't in any way want to offend Chris, his dad, or his family, but I'm Austin's mom and I should have a voice, too. It's also time to fast and pray. For the past three days I have been on a water fast and praying for the proper words to write. I had also given an open invitation for others to write letters as well. It was time to petition.

I wasn't expecting what happened next. The letters started pouring in from California to Maine, Massachusetts, Virginia, Georgia and many from Florida. It was amazing to read what was written on Alex's behalf. They were from attorneys, military officers, vets, even Austin's friends and some family members. It gave them a chance to have their voice and opinion heard concerning the charges against Alex. There were over 80 letters written; it touched my heart to read them.

There was something consistent in all the letters, words like *Austin wouldn't want this*. That was my driving force. The whole time from the very beginning I could hear Austin say in my heart, *I don't want this; stand by Alex, Mom*. The love that people showed in the letters made my heart warm. It was all about forgiveness. There were many different perspectives and viewpoints, but all written in love and forgiveness.

Everything is out of my hands now. I gave the letters that I had to Katrina and Lane and they will give them to Mac, Alex's attorney, and he will deliver them as evidence to the State Attorney's office. I have peace that I did what God led me to do. I'm sure that the people who wrote letters received a measure of healing because they were able to show forgiveness and help Alex in this way.

Alex flies back from California today to prepare for the trial. Hannah and I went to the Healing Rooms yesterday for prayer and it was exactly what we needed. His strength, His love, His guidance—God never fails to give us what we need. We may not understand everything, but we need to trust Him through it all.

We were invited to Lane and Katrina's home for dinner. I had been fasting for nine days, and it was time to end it. Alex brought a friend with him who works as a chef in California. He prepared an amazing meal for us! However, there is a three-hour time difference, and we were on their timeline. We didn't eat dinner until 11:00 p.m. The restaurant-quality key lime cheesecake was served at midnight.

Before Hannah and I left, I felt led to take out my anointing oil and pray for Alex. It was a very powerful moment. Then I asked Alex's dad to pray the Father's Blessing over his son. He asked me to lead him in what to say because he had never done it before. I know they are Jewish, and I know the implications of the Father's Blessing and their heritage from reading the Bible is extremely important and was very long overdue. They gave and received forgiveness of their past hurts from each other. They expressed love for one another. Wow! That needed to be done, and there was not a dry eye in the house. Alex's friend was clearly touched by witnessing this and said he had never seen anything like it in his life. I asked him if I could pray for him as well and, of course, with his consent we did.

In the morning they were to meet at the courthouse for a motion to dismiss the case. A Motion of Traverse was filed, and the case was not dismissed as we had hoped. But I had peace about it at the same time. The State Attorney had not given Mac the list of expert witnesses until ten days before the court date. The judge was not happy about that, so the trial date was postponed again to allow Mac enough time to interview those witnesses. Jared is going to be in basic training and will not be available. The trial dates were then set for November 30th beginning with jury selection and the trial to follow ending on December 5, 2015, which would have been my ex-husband's and my 28th wedding anniversary. (Ironically, tomorrow, June

21, will be Dan's and my 18th wedding anniversary).

Tomorrow is Father's Day. I'm sure it will be a very difficult day for all the fathers involved. In a week will also be the birthday of both Dan and Chris and Austin's dad, on June 28th. My ex- and Dan had been very good friends when they were teens and into their 20s, a friendship that I know Dan would love to see restored one day. It would have been good for them and for Chris to allow their friendship to grow in the remainder of our years, or at least be comfortable around each other. That's restoration that has been long overdue. Trusting God is the only hope for that one day.

Chapter 22

Peace and Love

CHRIS CAME HOME TODAY to play hockey with Dan. I love to watch them play together. I mentioned to Chris that Hannah was going to have a birthday in a few days and jokingly said, "She only wants an iPhone 6!" He said, "No! She's not even in high school!" The next thing I know he's calling me from the phone store and telling me to keep a number, that it's Hannah's new iPhone. He bought her a new phone and put her on his plan. What an amazing big brother Chris is! What a blessing he is to us!

The following Saturday I got a text from Chris at 12:30 a.m. It said that he had just run into his ex-wife. He was driving quite a long distance from his home and decided that he was hungry. Being late at night, he googled for good restaurants open at that time and found one close by. As he walked in and was being seated, his eyes were drawn across the room. There she was looking back at him. Not what he was expecting to see!

There she stood with a bride-to-be sash across her chest surrounded by all her friends, family, and her fiancé. Of all the places in the world and all the nights he has to walk in on her bridal party! I personally think it was a divine appointment for each of them to let go of any feelings that they had before she started her new life with her new husband. It was a bit of a release for both of them, and another reminder that God is in perfect control of everything. He guides us and directs our steps. He heals our wounded hearts and He gives us new beginnings.

The very next day Hannah and I went to the new mall nearby and had lunch at the Cheesecake Factory. As I looked across the restaurant, there was my ex-mother-in-law and her daughter that had come to visit. She must have been here to support the family for the trial that had been postponed. So, I sent Chris a text letting him know that they were at the same restaurant and asked him if he thought I should say hello to them. I didn't want to offend anyone or cause a scene in any way.

As I had glanced over just in time to see his aunt ending a phone call, I assumed Chris had called her, they quickly got their things and left. Hannah wanted so badly to say hello to them as she had been praying for them every single night and will continue to do so. She couldn't understand why they didn't like us or want to talk to us. It broke my heart, too. As we left, we saw them walking ahead of us at a very fast pace. So, we turned around and went in the opposite direction, as to not make them feel uncomfortable.

Every day we are given opportunities to make changes for the better yet avoid them because we don't want confrontation or to be rejected by people. I have a daughter to raise, and she is watching my example as I lead and teach her in God's ways. I will be accountable for my actions around her. As she gets older, if I want her to be a healthy and mature Godly woman, I better set the best example possible.

I am once again feeling tired and empty as my sister and her fiancé John are planning their wedding for August 22nd, our parents' 50th wedding anniversary. I am the maid of honor and I am not living up to the responsibility. I'm happy for them, but at the same time, the last thing I want to do is be around anyone who knows me. I want to stay away from groups of people, and I don't particularly want people to notice me. I feel like I want to just be invisible. I guess the fact that Austin is not here with us and we are moving on with our life—I can't see my family all getting together and that empty chair.... I want to avoid seeing that empty chair. I'm afraid of what I might have to feel. I guess I feel like my life is a bunch of sharp, broken pieces of glass or pottery. I just need to trust God as He puts all the brokenness back together into a beautiful mosaic picture. I trust Him with handling my broken pieces. He knows right where they belong. He makes all things new.

Forgiveness and love are two of the most powerful things that a person can give and receive. I have learned over the past year especially, that to some people it comes quite easily and to others it seems almost impossible. You see, it's a choice, one that comes directly from the heart. Not from reasoning in your mind, but an emotional response.

You can tell almost immediately, when someone has the ability to be moved with compassion as they are faced with difficult circumstances that require forgiveness and love to be demonstrated.

Just now as I looked out my window contemplating this, a long black snake slithered by me. It didn't fill me with fear as it once would have; I was just aware that it was there.

The opposite of forgiveness and love is obviously unforgiveness and hate. We can be keenly aware that they are working in the lives of people, even when they may not see it clearly themselves, but it is our job to constantly shine the light of Jesus through our lives over the darkness of unforgiveness and hate. We know that the light always expels the darkness. Jesus, being the light of the world, and His perfect love casts out all fear.

Chapter 23
Deposition

I ASKED ALEX IF I could talk with him, so he stopped by around 3:30 p.m. We talked for a while. I wanted to make sure he was doing all right. He hadn't seen Austin's headstone yet, so I drove him to see it. He saw firsthand the design I had created, the mirror image of what we had both etched on the back of the stone and also tattooed on his back left shoulder. I watched as he stood there and studied every detail.

As we sat out at Austin's grave, he told me how he had managed to get Austin to keep the apartment clean, which was a miracle in itself. He said that he had set a standard and told Austin, "When you are done with that throw the wrapper away," or, "Wash that dish when you're done with it" and he did it. I told him that Austin is now setting the standard for him to follow God and to let God lead him. He understood.

After having our talk, I let Alex have a few minutes to pray and talk to Austin. We headed back to my house where we all prayed together for healing and encouragement. Before Alex left, he was looking at a family photo when he said, "Austin always wore that FSU necklace." He asked me if I knew where it was. There were about three of them around that he had worn, so I picked one up from "Austin's table" and told him that I wanted him to have it. He thanked me, looked intently at it, then wrapped it around his wrist and held it tightly. He kept holding it tightly, I could tell it meant a lot to him. He also told me that after I had prayed for his chef friend and spoken the Father's Blessing over him, he called his parents and told them about it. He said that it was very emotional for him. I hoped that it brought him healing wherever he needed it. As Alex left, he met Dan in the front yard, and they spoke for quite a while.

I have given everything up to God and can't plan for anything because I forget everything five minutes after I think it. He can plan and order my day—that's putting my full trust and faith in Him! That's pretty much why I have been journaling everything - so I don't forget everything in the order that it has happened. Journaling also gives me permission to release the difficult details out of my mind and onto paper, it gives me peace and a clear mind.

July 27th, my mom's 76th birthday. My sister and I took her to get her mother-of-the-bride outfit and we had a wonderful time together. I am starting to see my mother's heart begin to heal, our loss has been very difficult for her and my dad.

[3] Praise be to the God and Father of our Lord Jesus Christ, the Father of compassion and the God of all comfort, [4]who comforts us in all our troubles, so that we can comfort those in any trouble with the comfort we ourselves receive from God. 2 Corinthians 1:3-4 (NIV)

I was awakened today by a loud clap of thunder and a heavy downpour of rain. Amazing flashes of lightning split the sky. I quickly got out of bed, made my coffee, and headed out to the back porch to admire God's display of power all around me. How I love the rain, the smell, the noise, the lightning! The rain cleanses everything it touches!

It was going to be a busy day. Dan stayed home from work today because he had received a subpoena for a deposition about a week and a half ago. Why Dan, we wondered. He had been mostly silent the whole time. He wasn't there the night of the accident. He doesn't just take the day off work unless it is something he has planned on his own well in advance. We couldn't figure it out until we got to the courthouse. I introduced Dan to Mac, and we took a seat outside the door awaiting the arrival of the State Attorney. I noticed that there were others there, detectives and witnesses, to give their depositions, also.

Then Mac said that there must have been a mix-up with his secretary. They had put *Dan* on the deposition instead of *Donna*, because I was on the witness list, not Dan. In a way I was glad that I hadn't known sooner. I would have stressed out over what I would say. This was much better for us all! I was glad Dan was there for moral support. I really needed him there with me, but he would have never even considered being there if it hadn't happened just this way!

Mac and I walked into the deposition room where the State Attorney was sitting, waiting on us. He turned on his tape recorder as we sat down and asked me to raise my right hand and swear to tell the truth. I was looking for a Bible to put my hand upon, but there wasn't one! Mac sat quietly the whole time, taking notes. The State Attorney didn't have a list of questions prepared to ask me. In fact, he didn't seem very engaged at all. It was as if he had something else on his mind. He just seemed to rattle off a few questions from the top of his head. I answered them truthfully to the best of my ability. It was over before you knew it and we were free to go.

I felt like there will be a breakthrough as I had been meditating on Psalm 143:1, *Hear my prayer, O* Lord; *listen to my plea! Answer me because you are faithful and righteous.*

When we walked out of the deposition room my heart was racing. I quickly found Dan. I really needed him to emotionally connect with me and comfort me. However, as I approached him, he was staring out the large picture window overlooking the city, trying to map out the best route to the post office to mail the package that he had in the car. Wow! Asperger's' at its finest!

Chapter 24

Public Speaking

AFTER WORK TODAY I drove out to the island and went up to Lane and Katrina's spa. They both happened to be there. We sat and talked for quite a while. I can't say enough about how it seems to help when we get together and share what's on our hearts. I know that it always puts things into a new, updated perspective for me. I shared with Katrina that I felt someday we will be telling our story in front of large groups of people. She didn't want to hear it but also felt that it was true.

Lane said that he had just told her that he wouldn't be surprised if someday we were going to be on the set of a National talk show! That's so funny. We both need to be delivered from fear of speaking to large groups then! God willing, we will have to start small!

We had talked before about women's weekend retreats at the spa. Whatever we are called to do, we will need to do it together, telling our story and being examples through our testimony. (I have already had a couple of opportunities to give my testimony in front of groups of women and pray with them on forgiveness.) Even if this doesn't come to fruition, talking about it got us through that difficult time with a purpose driving us in forward motion.

As time passes, I feel like I've been going through a purging, a letting go of who I once was, a releasing of my relationships and everything that made me feel comfortable. I am convinced more and more every day that what we have gone through had been planned long ago. As far back as when my boys were very small, I can see how dates, numbers, and certain experiences tie into the big picture.

I'm reminded of the time when the boys were baptized, they were five and eight years old. As the pastor prayed over Chris, he misunderstood me when I had given him their names and baptized him *Christopher Austin*! I was upset at the time because his fathers' parents were there, and since all three generations share the same middle name, I didn't want them to think we were being disrespectful. Now it's a beautiful memory.

The same is true of when Chris had graduated from High School and gotten married a month later, at 18 he had the privilege of having Austin be his best man. Also, the time when they ended up going to the same youth camp together because of a mistake I made of forgetting about Austin's kids' camp two weeks before. They got to spend that week at teen youth camp together. God has always been in the details.

My sister's wedding was a lot of fun and it was nice to have my family there. It was a very hot day and the wedding was outside. Unfortunately, my dad got overheated and a little overwhelmed with all the people. He had not been feeling well to begin with, so he ended up watching the wedding from inside the house. My brother John took the honor of walking Mary down the aisle, or across the grass if you want to be technical.

Everything was fine until they finished the ceremony with Adam Sandler's *Wedding Singer* song. It was the song that I made Austin practice over and over and convinced him to sing at my sister Ina and Steve's wedding reception. I had videoed it and we ended up playing it at his funeral. There was a bench nearby and I saw that Chris had made his way over to it. I walked up and sat down beside him, then he put his arm around me and we both just sobbed. We cried all the way through the song. I don't think anyone noticed us, but it was that *empty chair syndrome* that we were beginning to get so acquainted with. We soon wiped our tears away and carried on.

After a few family photos, Chris and my brother took my dad home to rest. The wedding and reception went well, considering the bride jumped into the pool in her wedding dress! So, what else would a bride do when someone spills red wine on your dress! It was amazing that her hair still looked good. I was her hairdresser for the wedding!

Chris called his father to come and pick him up toward the end of the night. We had a heartfelt conversation in the driveway as he sat in his car and had Chris in tears as we spoke about how amazing our boys had turned out and how proud I was of Austin and Chris. It was also ironic that at Mary's first wedding in 1991, I had announced that I was pregnant with Austin. They drove off to spend some time together.

In the morning, Dad still wasn't well and was having a hard time breathing, so he was admitted into the hospital. He ended up staying there for a week and a half. After having five stents put into his heart he was doing better, but he almost didn't make it through the surgery. We prayed the whole time because his lung capacity was only at 30% and had left him ineligible for heart bypass surgery. We were grateful for the surgeon and his staff. Dad ended up in a rehab for a couple of months, which took a toll on Mom. We are grateful to still have him and she was glad when he was well enough to come home.

It's my birthday today, and the girls took me out for breakfast with Hannah, too! We had a wonderful time and it happened again—I got the bill for Hannah and me, and it came out to $17 exactly. How does that happen? Hannah had wanted to order coffee and act grown up. She didn't drink it; she just wanted to load it up with sugar and cream. Perhaps that's why it came to $17 even. I kept the receipt and put it into my Bible to remember...maybe Austin is saying, Happy Birthday, Mom! I love you."

Chris had asked me a question the night of the wedding as we sat on the tailgate of his truck waiting for his dad. He asked me, "Mom, I want to ask you and Dad if I can speak for you both at the trial. I know how you both feel, and I know what you both want." Wow! What a question. You must really trust someone to allow them to be your voice in such a serious matter. I prayed about it for a week or so and concluded that I could trust my son to speak my heart because he knows it so well.

I remembered when Chris had asked me a question ten years earlier. I had to pray about it at that time as well. He had asked me to forgive his dad what he owed me in back child support to make his life easier because he had been so diligent and hardly missed a payment, but every once in a while, it was hard for him to keep up. About a thousand dollars a year had built up over 12 years, and I heard Chris' concern for him. Dan and I had agreed that it would be the right thing to do to just forgive him of that debt. So, I went to the bank with the forgiveness of debt contract that I had written up on my own, signed it, and had it notarized. I remember the notary at the bank saying, Wow! I don't think I could do that." I took it to the courthouse and filed it, making it official.

That's when I began to realize how powerful forgiveness is. I think it changed everything. We all have the power to forgive someone of something. A debt they owe, a wrong they have done, an offense, even when they did nothing to deserve it, but you do it anyway. It has this power to change things for you and the other person. It's always worth it to forgive.

After I reminded Chris of this memory from 10 years ago, I said, "Yes, you can speak for me in court (unless it is out of my control) because I trust you that much. I know whatever you choose to say to represent my voice, you will respect and honor me as your and Austin's mother."

He thanked me, and in a way, he had felt like he had more of the ability to keep peace in the courtroom. (He probably didn't want me to get too religious!) I'm sure that empowerment brought Chris some much-needed healing as well. (In the end, however, I did speak at the trial as I was called to the witness stand by the judge.)

Chapter 25

All Things Work Together for Good

I HAD BEEN SO slow at work and praying to God to bring me more customers. Then, in walked a man that needed a haircut! He said he is from out of town and only comes in for weekends to play guitar at The Island Reef Restaurant. That got my attention because Alex had been working there.

Once again, I believe God was showing me that all things work together for good for those called according to His purposes. He truly directs our steps. After work, while visiting my dad at the nursing home,

Mary had invited me to an annual barbecue party at the home of her husband John's best friend, so I went with her.

They were all talking about the trip they were getting ready to take. They had been offered a place to stay in Colorado for the week. Jared's family owns that home— Just when I thought things couldn't get any crazier Dawn's daughter showed up at this small barbeque get together and again, not a coincidence. All in one day, God was showing me that He is in perfect control and that He orders our steps as we keep our eyes on Him. It makes me wonder how much had been preordained before we lost Austin, and even how Mary and John met. She had walked past him in a restaurant, and they spoke briefly, but on her way to the car, she heard a voice speak to her twice to go back and ask him for his phone number. It was such a God thing, that she had to call me later that day and share with me that she thought she had heard God speaking to her! We are all so glad she listened!

The next day as we were leaving church, the pastor had sent someone over to get us when he recognized Mary and I from the week before when we had asked for prayer for our dad and I had also told him about losing Austin. He wanted to know how Dad's surgery went. He also wanted to introduce me to his wife in the connection center. There, standing with her was a good friend of mine that I had met at The Door meeting—it just kept on going! God kept bringing people across my path to continue to show me that He was in everything.

Hannah and I went to The Door meeting last night and got prayer. It was amazing to feel God's peace continuing to heal me. He just never stops, if you just let Him take the lead. Hannah and a couple of the other young girls were in the other room having their own prayer meeting. They were so transparent with one another, sharing the painful stories of their lives and trusting one another. That's rare to see kids getting real with one another, but that's when healing can take place, when you're not afraid to share and get it out.

As I was waking up this morning I was drifting in and out of prayer mode when I heard amplified, *Austin's last day!* I'm not sure what that will turn into. Maybe one day we will film a documentary of Austin's last day. It would be a powerful tool for opening youth talks. They would be able to relate to each of the segments throughout that day. It was a divinely orchestrated day that plays out like a movie, down to the last fist fight Chris and Austin had in the backseat, recorded by Alex on his cell phone. Even the last thing Austin purchased—a video game download—it's all there. We will wait on God to see. I don't want to take matters into my own hands and create a mess trying to help God out with the plans that I think He has for us!

One of my clients came in today. She's a single mom with two boys. I started doing her hair shortly before I lost Austin. She asked me, "How is that boy doing, your son's friend, Alex?" I told her that God is in perfect control and that he's going to be okay. He has the best defense attorney in town; God picked him out! She said wow, what's his name? When I told her, she was surprised. She said, "I only know one attorney in town and that's him! We are neighbors. I get their mail all the time and they get mine!" She told me how pleasant his family is. Once again God showing me that he is in complete control.

Katrina sent me a text to let me know that she and Alex were heading up to Georgia and asked me to pray for her father who was on a ventilator after a bad reaction to medication. I prayed and headed off to work.

I had that returning client from The Island Reef Restaurant come in. He said that he was sorry he had not put two and two together on his last visit when I had told him about Austin and about Alex being his best friend. He was very empathetic and sorry for my loss. I was able to encourage him as he told me about a God-experience that he had about a year ago that month. He let me pray for him and I broke out my special anointing oil, a gift I had recently received at The Door. I anointed his hands and prayed for God to bless his music and that when he plays and sings the atmosphere would change and people would be healed, set free, and delivered. I prayed that people would even come up to him and say, "Something feels different, more peaceful! I'm beginning to feel like myself again."

Katrina's dad is doing much better. He is recovering. And my dad was admitted to the hospital today with low blood pressure, of all things. After visiting him I was walking to my car when, out of the corner of my eye, I saw a friend of mine drive by. I called her and asked her why she was at the hospital. She said her sister was in the emergency room with high blood pressure and trouble breathing and that her sister Jackie was with her. (the one we had given the baseball to on Mother's Day.)

I headed in to visit them. We had prayer, then after a short visit, I turned to leave, but I heard a word audibly, *unforgiveness*. I turned around and told her what I had just heard. She said, "Yes, I know. I read that this morning on Facebook and I've been thinking about it all day!" I asked her if she was ready to get rid of it, and of course, she said yes. She had a box of tissues on her lap and we did a little "tissue therapy." She pulled out a tissue for each person she forgave and then threw it into the garbage can. When she was finished forgiving everyone, including herself and God, I had told her that it would have been hard for her to receive her healing with all that unforgiveness in there. So glad she decided to forgive—another divine appointment!

I went to visit my dad in the hospital today, and as I was walking in, I saw some people that I knew from the salon, they had been Jennifer's clients for well over 20 years. They were there to visit their father who was in the in the end stages of his life. I was thankful that Jennifer and I were able to pray with him the following day and say goodbye. He was on the same floor as my dad. We all stood around his bedside singing his favorite hymns, a private moment that we were able to share as we encouraged the family, some of whom were having a very difficult time. He passed through the Heavenly Gates that evening. Another divine appointment. (My dad was released from the hospital and went home the very next day).

I can't help but think that there was a purpose in my dad's short hospital stay to allow us to encourage others, to show our love and support, and to pray for their needs—another example of God working all things together for His good.

Chapter 26

Scavenger Hunt

CHRIS FLEW IN FOR a quick visit and to spend some time with us and with his dad's family, then flew out early the next morning to get to work on time. Before he left, he said that he had been thinking about buying a home here eventually and moving back to town. Nothing would make me happier and I'm sure his whole family would be elated. In the meantime, I will be praying for God to make a way. He shouldn't be so far from home. (As I am in the process of completing this book He has moved back, built a very nice house and has been blessed with an amazing wife and they have started a beautiful family.) Praise the Lord for answered prayers!

Mary had planned a night out with John to celebrate a friend's birthday the day before Halloween. However, after his commitment, he had forgotten that he promised his son a father-son day. She was disappointed at first as she explained to me that it was a scavenger hunt and she needed a partner. Before I knew it, I was saying, "Hey, chill out! I'll go with you; problem solved!" What was I thinking? Bar hopping on a trolley all night long! That's definitely not my thing. I'm not a big drinker! But I'll do it for some sister-time. I had all week to prepare.

Thursday night I went to The Door meeting and a wonderful couple from Bulgaria were there ministering. They have been at The Door a few times, and we are always so blessed to hear them teach the Word of God. He spoke a prophetic word over me and I'm going to be transparent here and share it with you. Somehow, I feel it is not only encouraging to me, but that those who read it may have a greater understanding that God sees us as we are, and he loves us. A prophetic word is for strengthening, encouraging and building up the body of Christ. Here goes—you must read this in a broken English and Bulgarian accent!

> Thank you, Holy Spirit. Donna, you are such a personality, so much joy, so much fun, you know, without words—you speak a lot. Your face, your laughing, it is Kingdom. Some people are coming to my country and they don't speak the language. They go to the gypsies. They love them; they hug them. And you understand they don't speak the language, but they speak already without words, and you have this personality.
>
> Father I'm praying for this woman. Father, I'm asking—everyone has challenges in this world. Even if we go through these challenges You will be with us. I'm praying, Lord, that You are blessing your daughter, blessing my sister. Thank You, Lord, for who she is. Thank You, Lord, for what You have done in her life. Thank You that she is Your child. Thank You for the great and mighty things you are doing in her life.

Lord, bless her. It's so sweet; it's very simple. You are the light. It's probably something you hear thousands of times. The Lord says, "I use you for your goodness, for your benefit. You can go to these places. You think you need somebody to help you, but when you minister to others you yourself are taken care of.

And He says that you are the light, and I saw that you are on the seaside. It's kind of dark, but your house is light. Some people are looking for the place to get to the light -blessings. Wow! What an amazing word!

Now I must share what happened the next day! The birthday party started off at our friend's house. Mary and I were a team for the scavenger hunt. There were 42 of us and we were waiting for the trolley to arrive to take us on this adventure. She had bought us matching Tampa Bay Buccaneer shirts since that was the theme of the night. As the trolley arrived, we were all prepared to get on when I was surprised to see that the driver was a good friend of mine from the church I had previously attended. We had taught the AG girls club together. It was great to see her again, so I sat close up front so we could catch up!

Several years ago, the guy she had been dating had found out that I had forgiven the child support arrearage and asked me if I could help him and his ex-wife write up a document to do the same thing. She wanted to clear that debt for him so he could move forward. He, like my boy's dad, was an excellent father and had given of himself over the years and deserved the break. If more people would choose to do this forgiveness of debt thing, they would find that they would have a better relationship from family to family. More respect and agreement came out of it which, if you ask me, is worth more than gold.

So off we went with our scavenger hunt list. It looked like fun! I had decided before we left that I wasn't going to drink as proof to the others in the group that you can still have fun without drinking. At the first stop we all got something to eat and began to look for the items on our list. The second stop came up and then the third, there we were at the Island Reef Restaurant and guess who was working there that night? It was Alex. Mary had told everyone on the trolley to make sure to show him that they loved and supported him and to tip him well. So, she and I went to surprise him first. He was really glad to see us. He hugged me so tight I could hardly breathe. He was so thankful for us standing by him and his family. We took a couple of pictures with him and off we went to find our treasures.

My sister and I started to look for a golf cart, so she led me into the trailer park across the street. I didn't want to walk through there, so I told her I was turning back. As I crossed the street a big strong muscular man dressed nicely with dark skin was driving slowly toward me, in a fairly new muscle car, stopped and rolled down his window. He told me if I wanted to get into his car, we could have some fun, and he'd really like to buy me a couple of drinks. I just looked at him and said, "No, I don't think so. I'm married and no!" Really, I couldn't believe my ears. The gentleman in the car behind him stopped and asked me if he had just heard what he thought he heard! "How disrespectful," he said, and I agreed.

I headed into a gift shop, found most of the scavenger hunt items on the list, and took my picture with each one. Soon I met back up with Mary and I told her about my crazy experience. We headed back to The Island Reef to find our last item on the list, which was someone wearing a college ball shirt. She began to walk around to the left, outside at the patio bar by the water. I stood by the door and followed her with my eyes. She stopped and began talking with this man, and I saw him motioning for her to sit next to him. I took a closer look and realized she was talking to the man that had tried to get me into his car! Now he was hitting on her; because we were dressed alike, he probably thought she was me!

I motioned to her that it was him and she said, "Excuse me, I think you are being very inappropriate. First you tried to get my sister in your car; now you're hitting on me! We deserve more respect than that, and you are treating us like dirt!" She began to back up, and just then he stood up, clenched his fist, and told her explicitly to shut up. The bartender had to take control of the situation.

Mary said, "That's okay, I'm leaving!"

He sat down and said, "Good because I was about to punch her right in the face."

Just then the bartender said to him, "That's it. You are barred. Don't ever come back here!"

It had become quite a scene that could have ended badly. We couldn't believe what had just happened as we walked back into the area where Alex was working. While we were telling him about the crazy situation, the Patio bartender from outside came in looking for us. She wanted to say thanks for finally giving her a good reason to ban this man. She had wanted to for months. She said that he was married and had small kids at home and hits on women there all the time. She went on to tell us that he had tried to assault her friend just a few weeks ago. She said he is a dangerous man. I know that was long-winded, but I believe God wanted that strong man to be removed and to be publicly embarrassed for his behavior.

I remembered back when I had prayed in the salon with the man who plays the guitar there on the weekends. I prayed for the atmosphere to be changed when he plays there. Something to think about. Just then, my sister spotted an older gentleman wearing a college baseball shirt, and off she went to get a picture with him. We were the second team done with the scavenger hunt!

She and I gave Alex a hug and headed off to get back on the trolley. I noticed earlier that the driver had a difficult time maneuvering that big trolley around the U-turn at the end of the street, so, she just made a right hand turn instead. We would drive right past the restaurant. As she came to the door of the Island Reef, I said, "Please stop right here!" The patio bar was off to our left and full of people with Alex managing the bar just inside to our right. She rang our trolley bell loudly and all 43 of us on board began yelling out, "Goodbye, Alex!"

Everyone on the trolley was pretty rowdy by then and had a few drinks in them, except for the driver and me! Then Alex waved back from inside, and you couldn't control these people! They began chanting *Alex! Alex! Alex!* They all were there to support him at that moment and knew what had happened to Austin and could tell he was a great kid working through very difficult circumstances. So, they all started yelling, "We love you, Alex!" He came out and stood there very humbled and feeling loved by people that he didn't even know. He was smiling for the first time in a long time. We rang the trolley bell one last time as we drove away.

The emotion in that trolley was so strong, it was even surreal. I think he really needed people to show him love, especially from my sister and me. We had to wipe the tears from our eyes because we knew Austin would have been so touched at the love and support shown to his friend.

Chapter 27

WOW!

THIS MORNING I WAS getting out of the shower, listening to Pandora music, and minding my own business when I heard this, *the strong man has been removed.* Wow! God showed me in the natural, just as what had happened the night before, the strong man had been removed. It has spiritual implications, too. I believe the strong man who has been known as Satan, who rules the darkness, has been removed from the situation for Alex. Then Alex was shown love and support—perfect love casts out all fear. (Okay, maybe I over-analyze things! Maybe...but I don't know.)

The seventh of November—happy 97th birthday to Mr. Billy Graham!

Austin's and Alex's friend, Rachel, had her beautiful baby girl yesterday. There is another story of reconciliation taking place. All these months Katrina and Lane had taken Rachel into their home after she found out she was going to be a single mom. Her relationship with her mom had not been very strong, so Katrina stepped in to become that friend for her—that mentor and motherly role model.

As the due date approached things didn't go according to plan. Katrina had to take an emergency trip to Georgia when her daughter, Ruthie, needed to have emergency appendectomy. So, Rachel's mom flew down from up North for the birth, and the baby's father decided that he wanted to be there for the birth, too. God was at work here bringing order, restoration, and creating beautiful memories that couldn't be forgotten. Little Emmy was born, would you believe at 6:07 pm. (representing June 7).

The last time I had seen Rachel was July 13 when Cheryl, Hannah and I had gone to Lane's and Katrina's home to baptize him in their pool. Hannah presented Lane and Katrina with fresh cut flowers, as I handed the communion elements to Lane. He said that they brought back childhood memories.

Ruthie had decided that she wanted to be baptized as well, Rachel and Katrina also agreed that they too would like to be Baptized! Wow, I wasn't expecting that! So, as we all sat around the living room talking about the significance and the meaning behind this decision, Lane had told me that he was prepared for baptism. His brother-in-law had been talking to him about it for a week and he was sure he understood what he was doing. For someone who was agnostic a year ago, he had come a long way.

So, as we all took communion, prayed together, and read a few verses from the Bible, after each shared what Baptism meant to them, we headed out to their pool. Katrina was first to be baptized. Then Ruthie decided that it was then her turn. Lane was next and last was Rachel, I know that being six months pregnant was a very special time for her and her unborn little blessing! When I was getting ready to baptize Alex's little sister Ruthie, I felt such a powerful wave of anointing come over me, I just knew that God had amazing plans for all of them, but it had gotten stronger for this beautiful young woman! I was honored to have had the opportunity to lead this beautiful family into this important fulfilment of scripture. Romans 6:4 We were therefore buried with him through baptism into death in order that, just as Christ was raised from the dead through the glory of the Father, we too may live a new life.

It was an amazing night. The only one missing was Alex, but I'm sure he will have his moment when he is ready. It will most definitely mark a day of healing for him. At first, I had told Katrina and Lane that I didn't feel qualified to baptize them, but they assured me that I was probably the most qualified person on the earth to baptize them. I had tried to drag them to Cara's and Gary's house (at The Door) and have them do it. Cara told me later that she would have had me do it anyway. That's how we feel sometimes, unqualified in so many ways. But do you know who does qualify us? It's Jesus Christ in us, that's who. I was blessed to be a part of this special time for them.

I went to The Door meeting last night. We had a special guest evangelist from England. He is such a character, so funny, and he also carries a very strong healing anointing, and has such an intoxicating personality in the Holy Spirit. Wow! He had told me that God had given me the WOW anointing! That made me laugh! He asked if I knew what that stands for. No, I didn't have a clue, but I knew that it was probably meant to make me laugh and be profound at the same time! The first **W** is for *Weird* because sometimes people think that I'm weird. (Which was true, I had always felt that way since I was very young) **O** stands for *odd* because I am odd, and I don't always fit in. (Also, very true!) And the last **W** is for *wonderful* because I am wonderful (I can't verify that one!)—that's the WOW anointing! That was fun hearing him at The Door meeting! Being a Christian can be fun, you know, and creative. I think the more I see the orchestration of things in my life fitting together, the more I understand this explanation, it's not to say I'm anything extra special, but the fact that when I recognize Gods fingerprints on the things around me and the divine orchestration of events as well as the weird and odd and wonderful connections, more often than not I hear people always tend to say wow! Wow! and wow!!

Chapter 28

Before the Trial

IT'S SATURDAY, NOVEMBER 21. The trial will start in a little over a week. As I woke up early this morning, I was having a dream. Mac was the biblical David and he took out Goliath with a smooth stone. Mac is not a tall man and certainly fits this description. I have a small smooth stone that fits perfectly in the palm of my hand. I had gotten it from a pile stones and rocks Mary had brought back from her last trip to Cape Cod this past summer. I think I'm supposed to give it to Mac at some point. I got up out of bed and turned on the TV, which I never usually do in the morning. And there was the caption. I think you guessed it—*Davey and Goliath!* There was my confirmation. Wow!

Tuesday November 24. After 17 months of having "Austin's table" collect memorabilia, newspaper articles, sympathy cards, keepsakes, guitar picks, pictures, scriptures, etc., I felt it was time to put it all away in Austin's hope chest in my bedroom. I felt strongly like it was finished, so by faith, I just put it all away; I had a peace about it, too. I closed the lid on the chest because I had done all that I knew how to do. It is all in God's hands and I trust him. I know that whatever happens is supposed to happen, and it will direct Alex on the best path laid out before him. I just sent Alex a text telling him that I would be with him next week at the trial. I told him that if he gets nervous to keep his eyes on me.

Hannah and I drove out to the spa to visit Katrina after stopping at the local donut shop and picking up a half dozen assorted donuts. We sat in her break room, enjoyed our snack and talked for quite a while. I have been very transparent in front of Hannah throughout this whole ordeal. I want her to see and hear our position of love and forgiveness toward Alex and his family. It's evident that she feels the same way, but everyone affected has the freedom to their own choice. To put it plainly, there is a line drawn in the sand. The clear choice that only your heart can choose to forgive or not to forgive. We enjoyed our time together.

Alex was meeting with Mac preparing for the trial. At the same time, the 80-plus letters were given to the State Attorney's Office on Alex's behalf, and we hoped that they would make a difference. God will work all things together for his good.

Wednesday, November 25—Chris called me as he had just landed at the airport and was on his way into town. He had learned that flying is a less stressful and quicker means of transportation then driving four hours each way. We talked for a little bit and he said something that made me think.

As I spoke to him about forgiving Alex and understanding my point of view, he said, 'Mom, I think it's all about what you believe;

it's your faith level." He went on to say, "Mom, to you Austin is in Heaven. You know it, so you have peace about it. I hope Austin is in heaven, and Dad sees him as dead, buried, and in the ground, stolen from him way too early." I get how they feel, my faith level had been set higher and I couldn't see it from their perspective until Chris explained this to me. Wow! Once again Chris gave me a new perspective to understand how they were seeing things.

We have been praying all along that the judge would be removed and replaced if it wasn't the right one. We had prayed Proverbs 21:1 NKJV over and over: *The king's heart is in the hand of the* LORD, *Like the* [a]*rivers of water; He turns it wherever He wishes.* I found out today that the judge who had the case was turning it over to another one. Mac told Lane that, if he could have handpicked the judge that has been appointed to the case, it would be the one that we got. Oh, the favor of God.

It's Sunday morning and the trial will begin tomorrow. I needed some encouragement. Hannah was a little under the weather, so she and Dan stayed home. It was a good opportunity for me to visit that familiar church that I had mentioned earlier in this story. As I pulled into the parking lot, Lane called to keep me up to date for this difficult week ahead. Whenever I speak to Lane or Katrina, I always feel better, grounded. There has never been anything major kept from me or concealed from me as far as the case is concerned. Complete trust, and even if there were, I respect the fact that Mac used wisdom in his representation and confidentiality of his client. (The family and attorney have shown me and my family nothing but complete respect in all aspects.)

As I walked into worship playing so beautifully, I quickly found a friend and sat by her, surprising her with my presence! (She had lost her husband just two years before on the same day that I had lost Austin.) The message about not letting the little foxes spoil the vines was very good. It was followed by communion.

When the service was over there was a call for prayer. I approached the pastor and the prayer team and asked for prayer for the upcoming trial. I gave a quick outline of the situation. The pastor held my hand and prayed with the baptism of the Holy Spirit and then inter-preted in English. The word that was spoken had been spoken over me before in the past, and it witnessed with my spirit now—that I didn't need to worry about what I would say in the courtroom, that God would fill my mouth with the words that I'm supposed to say, and not to worry.

Now sometimes when Christian leaders or prophetic people see a picture, or vision of something specifically for you, it can be easily interpreted with understanding for your edification to build you up in His strength. The pastor saw something that I didn't quite under-stand at first, but later through prayer, I understood. She said, "I saw a chalice—an old-fashioned, antique chalice put out in front of you." We both quickly understood a cup of affliction. Many other people wouldn't be willing to drink from this cup, and if they had a choice, they would not go through what I have gone through, and that God was with me. He will fill my mouth and speak through me. She said over and over that I was a living epistle.

Wow! What an encouraging word! Of course, I didn't understand what a living epistle was until I looked up the meaning. A living epistle is someone who through spending time in prayer, yield-ing completely to the leading of the Holy Spirit, and walks out the orchestration that God had for them to accomplish through their life. One who memorizes Scripture and proclaims the Word of God and has been transformed into a living breathing love letter from Christ. I certainly don't think of myself more highly that I ought to. It's humbling and for God's purposes, not mine.

Wow! How lovely. God is in us, through us when we learn to yield to him, and his plans unfold before us. We just have to get the flesh out of the way, and say, "Yes, Lord, I'm ready to be used by You. Lord, please help me to completely yield to Your will and be used for Your glory to touch people, reach people, help people, strengthen people, have courage, and to love and direct people to You."

I love this Scripture! I knew that I was supposed to go to this church today! I am ready for the trial to begin! I'm ready to walk through the persecution— through the glares from across the room—and just love them back and pray for them; they just don't understand.

Mac consulted with Alex and he had agreed to offer a plea for one year in jail and a felony to the State Attorney's Office. The State Attorney laughed at Mac and said he wouldn't be serious about a plea unless it was for more than ten years.

It's Monday night—today was jury selection. I spent the morning at my friend, Dawn's. We talked, drank, and prayed. We prayed for Austin's dad and his family members. We prayed for Chris, for his testimony not to offend his mother or his father, for peace to cover him as he had to relive the tragic events of losing his cherished and beloved brother. We prayed for God's love to penetrate his heart and comfort him. We prayed for Jared's testimony to be as accurate as he could remember. We prayed for all the witnesses to line up with the truth and for God's mercy and his grace to fill the courtroom, for peace to permeate the atmosphere. And we prayed for Alex to have hope for a future and to be able to fulfill the plans God has for him even though his life had now become so unfamiliar, so unrecognizable from who he once was.

Our prayer time was well spent today. I sent a text to Sarah, who had lived upstairs over Austin's apartment, letting her know the order of the trial throughout the week. She responded with surprise and a few concerns. The State Attorney's Office had left her a message on Wednesday at 4 p.m. and by 6 p.m. she had gotten off work and called to find the office closed for the Thanksgiving weekend. It had just reopened this morning. She knew nothing about the trial starting so soon. However, she was in Tennessee, and was also on the state's witness list.

She promptly called them and spoke to a secretary to ask why they thought she or her daughter would want to help his case when they don't agree with the charges. She said that she thought it was terrible what they were doing to these poor families. The secretary said, "Oh, so you should have been a witness for the defense then, not us? Yes, okay, she replied, I'll text the State Attorney at the courthouse and let him know. He's doing jury selection now. Have a good day."

That sparked a memory in me, of something that had happened to me many years ago. It was on Thanksgiving morning when I was about 25 and still married to the kids' dad. Chris was about four and Austin was one when there was a knock on my front door. It was a sheriff's deputy serving me a subpoena to appear in court. I was surprised and nervous at the thought of what was on the paper I was just handed. I was being falsely accused. I was being accused of scratching—keying—this girl's brand-new car in the grocery store parking lot just two days before. (The car that she had just gotten from a settlement in a lawsuit she had filed against her former employer for allegedly pushing her down on the ground in her workplace while pregnant.) I remembered seeing her alone, the client of my co-worker from the salon where I worked. She was illegally parked along the fire lane in front of the grocery store. I remember seeing her get out of her car as we were walking out of the store. I can still remember the angry look on her face when I smiled and said hello. I had just bought our Thanksgiving meal and had been teaching the boys about being thankful for all that we had. Chris was walking along beside me and Austin was riding in the basket of the cart. We loaded up our car and headed home. At the time we lived in the small condo complex right next to the one where Austin lost his life. In fact, we had taken them trick or treating through those very apartments. (When Chris started kindergarten his bus stop was right outside the entrance that I had pulled into that tragic night.)

So, yes, I went to the courthouse, and I didn't have any money for a lawyer to represent me. And because she had a witness to lie for her, I was found guilty and ordered to pay her $500 for a new paint job.

What I remember most from this was how devastated I was and felt that I now had a record, and I couldn't do anything to change it. It would be there forever, and it was untrue. That put me back into post-partum depression that I had just pulled myself out of with Austin.

When we got our income tax refund, half of it went to her and we decided that we would spend the same amount on something fun for us. So, we found two brand new One Design wind surfer sailboards, and in exchange for our disappointing loss, we bought them. We introduced our new sport to all our friends and enjoyed windsurfing over the next 20 years.

After I left Dawn's house, I decided to go to the courthouse and sit in the courtyard to pray. I drove there and parked along Main Street. As I walked toward the seating area, I ran into an attorney that Dan and I had known from holding season tickets to the Buccaneers years ago. He and his family sat in the row in front of us for many years. I told him why I was there, and he was sympathetic. He remembered that Austin and Chris had season tickets with their dad across the stadium and they came to see us at halftime every game.

After speaking with him, I made my way to a bench, and I began to pray and get acclimated to the atmosphere. I found the longer I sat there, the less nervous I became. I'm sure the prayers helped. I just people watched, and I witnessed things that probably go on there each day unnoticed.

I saw a woman, an addict, come out of the courthouse and head for the garbage can next to me. As she rummaged around in it her attention was drawn to the man sitting on a bench near me. He said to her, "Are you looking for this?" And he held up a blue plastic con-tainer. She said, "Yeah, man. How did you know?" He handed her stash to her and without incident, she pulled out her currency to thank him—three cigarettes—he accepted just one and put it behind his ear. She happily walked off. As police officers and lawyers walked past this unnoticed interaction they were clearly about their own business. Part of me wanted to jump up and talk to her and pray for her, but something told me that she had no plans of changing her ways at this time.

I noticed around me there were people wearing stickers that said *Juror* on them. I couldn't help but wonder if any of them were being chosen for our trial starting in two days. Sitting there by myself, it helped me understand the whole trial process. I was careful not to interact with any potential jurors. After a while I headed back home. Chris came home for the remainder of the week. We clearly had our own roles to play throughout the trial. There was no mistake that I was there to support Alex through the process, but I also supported Chris and respected his point of view.

Chapter 29

The Trial

As I arrived at the courthouse Wednesday morning along with Dan, Dawn, my sister, Dan's parents, and other family members and friends, I knew it was going to be a very difficult week. There was tension between the two sides of the courtroom. Austin's dad and his whole family sat off to the right behind the State Attorney's team, while we all sat to the left side of the room behind Mac and Alex. Each day I sat directly behind him with an empty row of seats in front of me reserved for witnesses.

Chris sat off to the right and in that last row each day by himself. He had created his own plumb line and walked it like a tightrope. I have such a respect for him having the utmost respect for each of his parents, while being true to himself at the same time.

The first day, as the jury was introduced, I was surprised to see one young man and the rest women. There were two women that were alternate jurors. The first day it was up to the State Attorney to prove his case. He had his expert witnesses testify. One was a Glock gun expert that had analyzed Alex's gun. There were a few others, but none that could prove that Alex had culpable behavior that evening that resulted in Austin's death.

When they played the 9-1-1 emergency call recorded that night, there wasn't a dry eye in the courtroom. Chris had quickly left the room before the tape began, and I was glad that he didn't have to relive those moments. I watched as Alex dropped his head while he listened to his own terrified voice, pleading for help. He admitted that he had shot his friend and that it was an accident. He was the first one to call and he took responsibility from the moment it happened. For the first time it was revealed to the whole family, the sorrow of the young man responsible for Austin's death. I believe it was that piece of evidence that moved them with the slightest bit of compassion toward Alex and maybe even toward me. We all endured through the recording; to the jury and judge, it was clear that we were all hurting.

Mac had pointed me out to the jury as the mother of Austin at the start of the trial and they occasionally looked at me for my reaction at times throughout the trial.

We were released to go for the day, and I asked Chris to pick up Hannah from school. She loves it when he's in town and can take her or pick her up from school. He took her to Starbucks and headed home. I waited at the courthouse to talk to Mac outside. I told him that I had something for him as he held out his hand and I gave him the small smooth stone. It fit perfectly into the palm of his hand. He looked puzzled, of course, and I told him that while I had been praying, I had felt God had shown me that he was like a David, and he took down Goliaths, and that I was to give him this stone. I told him that David became king one day and that I wouldn't be surprised if one day he was a judge! He laughed and told me that people had been telling him that he should be a judge, and that he would be a good one. It was fitting for him as tomorrow he was to come back and take down the Goliath in the courtroom (the strong man).

The next day came rather quickly and I was nervous because I was a witness for the defense. The next day Chris had testified and was truthful and neutral as well. I remember thinking he had the power to crucify Alex and that would be it—the brother. After all, he had been there with the boys throughout that whole day. But I never have been prouder of him as he continued to walk that perfect plumb line of truth and respect from the witness stand. From Austin and Alex playing guitars most of the night to his being asleep on the couch when the gun went off behind him and woke him to the devastating end, he gave his account of that evening. His maturity was revealed to all in the courtroom as he spoke.

After Chris had spoken, I left the courtroom and took a break. I met Jared out in the hallway where he stood with the attorney, I imagine his father had provided. I asked him how he was doing, and he said he was okay, just a bit nervous. I asked him if I could pray for him, and he said yes. I held his hand and prayed for God's peace to fill him and for God to guide his words and for his anxiety to go. I hugged him and he thanked me. Later, as he sat there on the witness stand, he did quite well and answered the questions to the best of his ability. He had mentioned that he wasn't paying attention to what was going on because he was playing video games and the volume was turned up as the gun had fired.

During lunch break, several of us including Dawn, my sister and I went to O'bricks on Main Street. While they ate, I went to my car to put quarters in the meter, drank some water, and had a handful of matzo crackers. I had been fasting all week during the trial. On the way back, I ran into three women, friends from the church that we had left. They prayed for me right there on the sidewalk. Afterwards I had noticed some of the jurors coming from the restaurant where we were standing and wondered if they had witnessed us praying outside the window. When I had returned to the table where the girls were, my sister had told me that she had ran into the pastor of the church that we now attend and asked him to pray with her also! God had us covered up one side of the street and down the other. I was very thankful!

As I walked toward the courtroom the next morning, I passed Austin's grandparents and for the first time I had gotten a smile and a hello. I tried to smile back as I walked by. I sat with my friends, Lane, and my family, then my heart began to beat fast and hard as I realized my time to speak was approaching. The judge had made the decision to allow me to speak. Mac had told us later that it was the first time in his 20-year career as Defense Attorney that the mother of the victim had gotten up to testify on the witness stand for the defense.

I approached and sat on the witness stand with the approval of the judge. He said that my testimony would be a reflection, or an understanding, of Alex's behavior the night of the accident. Mac asked me some questions, and I answered him to the best of my ability. I had a soft, quiet voice as I spoke into the microphone. I didn't look at Austin's dad's family; I just kept my eyes on Mac. He asked me about my relationship with Alex and I said that he had been to my house quite often with Austin growing up and that they had known each other since middle school. Then I said something that I know was from the Holy Spirit, He asked what our relationship was, and I responded with "We respect each other as human beings." I gave an account of my encounters with Chris, Jared, and finally, Alex, that evening. The State Attorney didn't have anything to ask me, and I was free to go. I was so glad when I finished testifying.

Mac called a couple of detectives up on the stand, and a gun expert from Colorado that taught on the Glock gun and all that concerns it. I don't want to get too far into the trial, and I may have some of my facts out of order because I didn't journal as much in those days during the trial. It was too emotionally exhausting, and it was all I could do to hold myself together.

I mentioned to Lane that it would help Austin's dad and his family in their healing process if Alex was given an opportunity to publicly apologize to them for the pain and suffering that he had caused them. He said absolutely and that he would mention it to Mac.

Thursday, December 3—the final day of the trial was coming up quickly. With it being Thursday night, you know where I went. Yes, to The Door meeting. I needed to get on my knees and pray for God's perfect will. I put my trust in Him! Several people prayed for me and for everyone involved in the trial. They prayed for both families of Austin, that emotional healing would come for Chris, for his dad and stepmom, and for his parents, family and friends as well. They prayed for Alex and for his family and for God's mercy and grace to fill the courtroom the next day for the trial verdict so that we can all move forward with our lives and put this difficult time behind us.

It was finally Friday morning we were all there at 9 a.m. for closing arguments. But first the judge called for the two alternate jurors. He thanked them for their service and gave them each a certificate, then invited them to stay for the ruling of the trial. The jurors came out and sat behind us. The State Attorney gave his closing statements and then Mac stood to give his. He had done an amazing job representing Alex. He paused briefly a couple of times and looked at his notes. Later he told us that he was shaking and didn't know why. He said in all his 20 years as an attorney he had never shaken like that. Mary told him that was because Donna and Dawn were in the room and they had been praying!

The judge called for a recess for lunch during the jury deliberation. We split up to go eat. Dan and his dad went to Jimmy John's for a sandwich. The State Attorney and his partner were there eating, also. Dawn, Mary, and I went to O'Bricks. I drank water and had a few matzo crackers from the zip lock bag in my purse as I continued my fast. I didn't want to be too weak. Dawn's son's girlfriend Jen met us there on her lunch break.

I had just mentioned that if it takes a long time it's not good, but if they have a verdict fast, it's good, right? We agreed that was correct, and almost immediately, Dan was calling me to say there was a verdict. We were all quite surprised and jumped up just as lunches were being delivered to the table. Jen agreed to box them up and pay the bill as we hurried back to the courtroom.

We ran into the two alternate jurors on the way and told them that the verdict was in. They began to walk with us. They told us that they knew how they would have voted if they were still on the case—not guilty! Hearing that made me feel hopeful. We were almost to the courthouse when my sister noticed that she had forgotten her purse at the table. We called Jen and had it kept safe for her.

As we walked up to the courtroom the alternate jurors were in tears as we talked. They said it had been very emotional being part of this trial. They chose to sit on our side in the back row. We were all there for the defense side of the room. It was evident that the State Attorney did not prove his case for the charges he had filed.

Chris came into the room and sat alone. When asked if his Father's family would be there for the reading of the verdict, he made a phone call, and said to wait, they were coming after all.

One of the bailiffs told Dan when he had gotten to the courtroom that it was going to be not guilty, that he had been through enough trials that it was clear to him. Austin's dad and his family came into the room and sat. Alex, Mac, and Mac's partner stood as the verdict was read. The judge had warned us all to be respectful of each side as this had been a very sensitive case for all involved. We all had already agreed to be calm and quiet whatever the verdict would be.

The judge had mentioned to the attorneys that this had been the smoothest case he had seen in a very long time. They all agreed that it was. As he read the verdict it was NOT GUILTY. What we had hoped to hear! However, there was an empathetic loud *Yes!* that came from the back row that was much too loud. Just then the judge reprimanded whoever it was. At first the judge thought it was Mary, but it was one of the alternate jurors that was now hiding in the back row. At that, Austin's dad and his wife promptly left the courtroom followed by Chris and the grandparents.

Chapter 30

Forgiveness & the Road to Closure

I<small>T WAS OVER</small>. I gave Dan a hug as we all embraced, marking the end of a difficult journey. Alex gave Mac a hug and thanked him. He also hugged his dad. It's amazing how Alex and Lane had restored their relationship throughout this past year and a half as their whole family drew strength from one another and from God.

Lane called Katrina right away. She was gathered with their family and daughter, Ruthie, in Georgia, as he gave them the verdict of *not guilty*. She said that when she hung up, they all just cried until they couldn't cry anymore. It was all over, and it was all just beginning at the same time.

I walked over to Alex and he hugged me and thanked me for standing by him. It was the one thing that kept him from falling apart. As we stepped out of the courtroom, Alex was approached by two bailiffs who said, "We don't usually do this, but we want to shake your hand, son. Good luck. It took a lot of courage for you." Alex was clearly humbled.

As we all met outside the courtroom door in the hallway, Lane asked if we could hold hands together and pray. He asked me if I could lead the prayer. Of course, I said yes. Mac, his assistant, Alex, Lane and their family, friends, and my family were all there—17 of us in all. My prayer was giving God thanks for His mercy and grace. Then I prayed Jeremiah 29:11 over Alex's life. "We know the plans You have for his life, Lord, for a hope and a future, not to harm him, but to prosper him. He has called upon Your name and prayed to You. You have listened and brought him back from captivity." I asked God to bless Mac and to continue to work through him, in Jesus' name.

We had to retrieve my sister's purse, so we all agreed to meet at O'Bricks, the very restaurant Dawn was at the night of the accident. The hostess pushed the tables together so we could all sit as a group. It was time to end my fast and I ordered a cup of soup. To be honest, I just wanted to relax and take a deep breath. It was bittersweet for me praying Jeremiah 29:11 for Alex to have a hope and a future when Austin's future, on this earth, was gone. But I know in my heart that he already has fulfillment in eternity. His legacy will now become "Austin's Harvest", those brought into the kingdom through his life, death and testimony as far as it can reach. The hope in Christ fulfilled in him for all eternity—where one day I will catch up with him, my sweet boy.

As Mac ordered lunch, he called me over and explained to me that he was not celebrating in any way and he wanted me to know. I told him that I understood and that I knew he wasn't, that it was the completion of months of research and lots of hard work, late nights, and early mornings.

We all sat and talked and ate. I asked Mac if he knew the story of David and Goliath. He said he knew it vaguely. I told him a quick version and encouraged him to read up on it himself sometime. I'm sure he'll figure it out. I also had asked him if the judge, who came out of retirement to take this case was related to the family who owned the farm where Mary and I had stopped on the way home from visiting Chris months before and he said yes, he was pretty sure that he was.

Chris headed back home right after the trial ended. Before we all headed over to the restaurant there was one newspaper reporter that was waiting for an interview. I was glad to see that the media had dissipated to just her. Armed with just an iPad, she stood outside the courthouse doors in the very spot where I had once prayed with Mac. The wind was blowing stronger than usual as Alex and Mac stood side by side. She recorded the video of Alex first thanking Mac for all he had done to represent him and then giving an apology to Austin's family and friends and to everyone that had been affected by the loss of Austin. He stated that he was happy about the outcome but had to live with this the rest of his life. This recorded statement was then quickly posted to the newspaper's website.

December 5—the next day Hannah and I had been invited to a women's tea by Ellen, Jon, Kate and Jakes mother. I really needed that! I knew who the guest speaker was and had heard her many times. I really wanted her to pray for me and I needed it, so I prayed for favor from God. Out of the room full of beautifully set tables, guess where she and her mom were sitting? Yes, at our table because it was next to the podium!

As she began to speak to the women there, she was saying things that were touching my heart and then it just happened—the floodgates opened, and I just lost it. The tears started flowing and I couldn't hold them back. She saw me and asked me to come up. She said God was healing hearts. She said a wonderful prayer over me, and she told me that this Christmas was going to be better than I had ever imagined it would be.

As I went back to my seat, I gave Ellen a hug. She had walked with me through this, too. Her son was Austin's first roommate; her daughter was the 9-1-1 dispatcher. Austin was like one of her own. I could tell that she had kept avoiding eye contact with me earlier. She confided that she was holding back her own tears. If she saw me cry, she was going to cry also.

December 11 has rolled around. Alex called me a few days ago to ask for Austin's dad's phone number. I prayed that it would go well as they speak to each other. I had no idea how he would react to Alex's call, but I hoped that they would both be able to handle it okay.

Wow! I just got another call from Alex. He just got off the phone with Austin's dad and they had a surprisingly good talk. He said he was a little taken back when he realized who was calling him. Alex told him how sorry he was about what he had done, and that if he could take it back, he would. My ex- said he knew it was an accident and that he didn't mean to do it. He said he didn't understand why they had been playing around with guns. Alex said he wished he could take it back. Alex also said he will never forget what he said to him at the family and close friends viewing, about doing something great with his life for Austin. What a blessing, a form of forgiveness beginning to take place in a father's heart, an answer to prayers.

After we had hung up the phone, he received a call from Austin's stepmom. She had called Alex to tell him that it took a lot of courage for him to call her husband. She also wanted to tell him that she was sorry for the way they had treated him throughout the trial. She said when she heard the 9-1-1 call she broke down in tears and realized that it had been an accident and that he didn't mean to do it. She also told him that as she watched the video, he had recorded for the newspaper she had cried again when she saw how sorry he truly was. She told him that they wanted to know how he was doing and to check in with them periodically. Breakthrough and answer to prayers! Thank You, Jesus! Having forgiveness doesn't minimize the offense; it just sets you free from the pain of holding on to it.

Chris has been a bit distant from me. I'm sure it's going to take a little time for him to get past everything. I'm praying for his healing and I know that he loves me!

My pastor was preaching today on forgiveness, yes that's a *now* word, it always is. Did I minimize the offense by forgiving so easily? I was wondering if I have done that. Do others think that I have? When you walk out your faith with forgiveness and just trust God with his plan, things have an opportunity to change as God will work all things together for His good. You may not like what happens in the testing and trials of your life, but if you don't trust God through the circumstances, you'll most likely fall apart. Guarding your heart through those difficult moments in life is so important. If you let doubt and unbelief into your heart a change can take place rather quickly, unforgiveness can turn into bitterness to poison you and alter the way you lead your life. Forgiveness is not saying that every-thing is okay, but it is saying, "I trust you, God, even when it's not."

That is not minimizing the offense or even my loss, which has been great. I choose not to camp out at the place of the offense, where one can easily become a victim. It must be so hard for Chris to get through this step of forgiveness, because the value of Austin's life is so great, the loss is so great, and his loyalty to Austin as his protec-tor and lifelong friend is real. I'm sure it's difficult for him to forgive so easily and quickly. I know it may be a process for him, and he has every right to deal with it however he chooses. But true freedom will come through true forgiveness ultimately, and through God's grace, mercy, and His love is the most painless way.

December 18—I headed over to see Katrina and Lane at the Spa. I had not seen Katrina since before the *not guilty* verdict. She had just arrived back home, and I needed to give her a big hug. We talked for about an hour and a half about what God had done, is doing, and is going to do. I think we are being prepared for what God is bringing us to do next.

Last night Cara and Gary held a black-tie Christmas party at The Door. Hannah had an opportunity to wear her flower girl dress from Mary and John's wedding! We had an amazing time of fellowship,

God's word, worship, and prophetic ministry. The Door has been so instrumental in my healing process and the intercession of the others has poured out into our lives all around me! It's amazing!

Five days before Christmas and we finally got a tree! With minimal decorations this year and a beautifully decorated tree, we are ready for the holidays. I remembered the word that the speaker at the tea had spoken to me, that I was going to have a better Christmas than I had ever imagined, and we did just that. Chris catered Christmas dinner from Carrabba's. I picked it up on Christmas Eve and heated it all up in the morning.

Chris had driven here in my new car on Christmas Eve! He blessed me with the down payment and even paid for the insurance. In true Christopher form, he only made me drive around with an expired tag for a couple of weeks until he could figure out where the tag from my old car ended up after he had driven it back home for the trade-in. That's Chris! I love my new car. I even got to pick out the color. I guess Chris isn't mad at me anymore! I love him! It truly was going to be a better Christmas than I had imagined it would be!

My sister and her family who live in Maine are here. What a blessing! They went to church with us today. The message was about not being afraid, or it will hold you back.

New Year's Eve—Austin's birthday. He turned 24 in Heaven. He is getting to see the fireworks from a Heavenly perspective! I love you, my sweet boy! Matthew 20:16 says, *the last shall be the first, and the first last, for many are called but few chosen.* He was born the last baby in our county in 1991. He was the first in our immediate family to enter the Kingdom of Heaven. He was called and chosen. I love him, but not more than the Father loves him! As I sit here writing, my thoughts travel with the noise of fireworks outside my window. Hannah and I stopped by his graveside earlier and put yellow carnations in a vase and watered the plants I had put there a few weeks ago. Hannah put her arms around Austin's stone and gave him a two-armed hug.

I have been feeling so tired lately. I feel like I just want to run away. Did I say run away? Oops! I meant get away! The church is having a women's retreat soon. If I am meant to go, God will provide and fill up my book at work with appointments.

Wow, God did it! I went to work, and every timeslot was filled. By the end of the week, I could pay all my bills and afford to go to the retreat! It must have been meant to be! Thank You, Lord!

It's January 15 and I'm at the women's retreat! It's as if God knew it was the end of the tribulation and trial; He didn't waste any time bringing me into His rest. I have been having an amazing time of healing, restoration, refreshing, and I'm meeting new friends, too.

We were broken up into small groups of about eight women and we got to know each other quickly. Our group leader just happens to have been Hannah's math teacher last year at the private school! There was another young woman I met that had the same last name as the judge. I could tell her and her mom's reactions to my story were more personal to them than they could divulge, so I respectfully never asked if she was related.

I was able to get up during the time of ministry and share a portion of my testimony in front of the whole group of women. We had a wonderful outline for the weekend, and it made me think about the plans that Katrina and I had been talking about, a retreat weekend for women for emotional healing and refreshing someday.

I spoke with Alex the other night and he told me that he was planning on coming back to Florida from California. He said he feels like God is leading him back here! What courage this kid has. He could live anywhere in the United States, even Georgia, but he wants to come back here where people will know who he is and what happened. He's going to be okay. Alex had to come home to face life head on before moving back up to Georgia with his family.

Chris had blessed me once again by getting me into another car with six months to go before the three-year lease ran out on my car. Now, I was getting a new car just in time for my birthday! At the dealership, while I was waiting for all the paperwork to be completed, I heard, "Excuse me, Ma'am," coming from behind me. I had turned around to see that one of the salesmen that works under Chris wanted to tell me something, so I stepped over to talk to him. I was thinking, "Oh great, what did he do now?" I sensed that he had been arguing with himself whether to approach me or not. He seemed to be around my age. He began to give me the greatest compliment that a mother could receive!

He said, "You did a great job raising your son. He is honest, has integrity (which is not something you always find in this line of work), and he's smart! If he ever leaves here, I'm going with him!" He went on to say, "You should be proud of him; you did a really great job with him!" Of course, I am truly very proud of him! I thanked him for the compliment and back off to work he went! Honesty and integrity and intelligent what a wonderful compliment.

Chris and Keila had a beautiful house built and are starting a family. I know in the time that he was with us that I had witnessed his healing process, his heart and mind has been transformed by the love and prayers of both his family and friends. I am so happy that he has decided to stay here with his family! Chris had previously taken Hannah and I down south to meet Keila's family. What a joy that was; what a beautiful family. I am beginning to see the next chapter of his life and it looks amazing! Keila is my long-awaited answer to prayer for Chris!

Something amazing had caught my attention! This past June 7th our nephew and his wife had their baby 5 weeks prematurely, Kyler was born on the anniversary of Austin's last day, around the same time that Austin had taken his last breath 5 years earlier to the hour, the new baby had taken his first.

We are expecting another miracle baby due on or around the first of June! Yes! Chris and Keila are expecting! Wow, that's another answer to prayer, I can't wait to become a grandmother for the first time!

I had a dream shortly after finding out about the pregnancy, it was early in the morning just before waking, I saw Austin in his heavenly body standing right next to Jesus, he was holding this beautiful baby, I watched as he kissed the baby on the forehead and passed him to Jesus and to the Father, then of course came the humor! Austin began dancing around in a circle singing I saw him before you did, I saw him before you did!!! I imagine its God's way of working all things together for his good, replacing the anniversary of a traumatic memory with yet another miraculous one. Once again … His timeline. Praise God for His signs and His wonders!

Chapter 31
Blueprints

I WAS REMINDED OF something very significant
that had happened in the year 2000. I can
see now how hyper focused I had been!
Three years before Hannah was born, my
coworker Jennifer and I were at the salon
when her client, Barbara had come in with
a set of blueprints. She was a teacher at the
same location of Hannah's private school.
At that time the school was going through
some changes that eventually resulted in
its closure and left it vacant for years. She
loved kids and felt a strong desire to build

and open her own school. She asked us to pray with her over the physical set of blueprints for God's perfect will to be done, for provision and favor through the process every step of the way. I didn't realize that I was praying into the blueprint of Austin's, Alex's, John and Jared's destinies.

It was a few years later, in 2003, that Austin was really struggling in school and I had asked Barbara, if Austin could attend her school with his McKay Scholarship and she quickly accepted his application. I was excited for him to have the opportunity of a small private school. Austin and Alex, Jared, John and countless others met and quickly bonded, and I had a strong feeling that they would someday impact the world and I was so right.

Losing Barbara, a couple of years later to lung complications while the students all attended the school's prom was devastating to us all. Some of the children stayed and graduated from that school and some went on to other schools.

Austin spent his last two years at the same public school Chris had graduated from, stepping right into his brother's footsteps in the media center. With the daily video announcements, he soon became a familiar face and his fun personality came to life! He did well in this new environment where his smile lit up the world! Ironically, that small private school Barbara started has moved a few times over the years and is now located on the same property as our salon and right around the corner from Hannah's school. I feel like it's a picture of everything coming full circle.

My sister Susan and her family in Maine are doing well. Her children are now in Bible college, and she is publishing a series of children's books that God had downloaded her with so that she can step into what He has put on her heart and called her to do. Share the good news of Jesus Christ and to teach truths and character lessons to children! She has even done several local radio interviews.

My other sister Ina and her husband Steve have moved to Florida leaving the cold snowy weather for good! Having two sisters living here in the nursing field will be a blessing for Mom and Dad in the near future as they get older and may require additional help. What an honor it is for children to be able to take their training and give the respect and care due their parents. Steve is a master craftsman and will have his work cut out for him as well, as he attempts to restore the 100 + year-old house that is our family home!

A short time ago, during the month of August, I was at The Door when I had received a text asking me if I could talk. I stepped outside and made the phone call. Remember earlier when my pastor's wife and I were painting the Noah's Ark mural at the church? We had discovered then that my son, Chris, who was 25 at the time, and her sister Sherry, worked together at a small car dealership, *it's a small world*, we thought!

But I knew God was doing something then, and he was now connecting the dots for something bigger. I was asking God, "What are You doing now? What are you trying to show me?" Well, now I know, or I think I do!

I called Sherry and we spoke for about an hour. I remember her asking me, "How do you do it, Donna? How do you breathe when you've just lost your son? How can I live without my son?" Her son was 17 when he had been shot and killed just a few days before the phone call. Now she had begun to walk through the same tragedy that I had. The circumstances are always different, but the pain is the same. Now she was "joining the club" that I wouldn't wish upon any parent to be the member of. I just shared with her from my heart some of the things that helped me get through each day.

I know now why our paths have crossed. I believe God is trusting me to help walk His broken daughter and her family through this difficult time in their life and into the peace that only comes from the Father. The healing path that the Lord has begun to lead us down has been an opportunity to reveal His light to others, to guide us into complete healing, I'm not completely there yet, but I am well on my way. That is what this book is supposed to be about, not just to tell my story, but to be able to reach out to mothers, fathers, and loved ones in their loss and direct them to the Father, to bring them encouragement and to give them the strength that they will need to survive, to help teach them how to breath when the wind had been knocked out of their sails.

My joy is full again, Chris and Keila just brought baby William home from the hospital today, and yes you guessed it, on Pentecost Sunday I got to meet my first grandson and he is perfect in every way. His due date was to be on Alex's birthday, the Monday after Pentecost. A true picture of the circle of life, As I bring Austin's Harvest to completion on this Monday after Pentecost I am once again reminded of the signs that follow us as we put to rest those things which are behind us and press on. We had to lay to rest our sweet cat Bella tonight, as yet another reminder of Gods perfect timing in all things and the true meaning of beauty for ashes. As we prepare to walk through the first week of June and all of the emotions and memories it holds, we are reminded that joy comes in the morning. The powerful testimonies that are written within Austin's Harvest reveal the building of a strength and faith that can only come from God. Chris and Keila continue to walk in this strength and faith of the Lord as they bring little three-month-old William home from the hospital today, the day after having brain surgery, we rejoice. Yes, of course, it's on my birthday. The most amazing thing is unfolding. I spoke with Katrina last night and what she shared with me revealed the fruit of receiving forgiveness. Last year they had a break in, in fact it was a neighbor's son high on drugs that had trespassed and upon breaking a window, he severed a finger on the broken glass. He bled so much throughout his rampage as he utterly destroyed their home, breaking everything in sight. It looked like a murder scene right out of the movies. Later that night Alex came quickly to his mother's side as his dad was out of town. After the investigation, they were escorted into the house by police officers and surveyed the devastation. Later that next day Alex asked his mom, is that what it looked like when you went back into the apartment with Austin's family? Not at all she replied. She was able to replace his memory of what he had imagined we witnessed that day with the truth. A whole year has passed, the young man's trial is coming up. They had been called to the DA Office on the 27th of July 13, 2021 (my mother's birthday and also Katrina's father's) The DA asked Katrina one question. Do you want him to go to jail? She could hear God speak to her heart "Do you believe, do you trust". Her answer was profound. No, I don't. We want him to get the help that he needs. If possible, to join a program for substance abuse so he can have a fair chance in life. She shared with me how it felt to her. She said when she was in that moment, she had to choose, do I extend forgiveness? Wow! When you choose to forgive, it feels good... it feels better... it gave her a sense of peace.

Our grief has become our sword!!

About the Author

My mother lives her life for Christ. Her walk with Christ is not an extension of her, it is her. Selflessness is at the core of who my mother is. Whether it was raising my little brother and I as a single mother early in life, or today as a leader and mentor at Our Fathers House, a Christian ministry that helps single mothers. My mother has always lived her life to serve others and ultimately to serve Christ. I have witnessed my Mother's faith grow from a seedling into a forest of Redwoods over the past 25 years. The strength and the grace my mother displayed in the worst days of her life will live with me for the rest of my days. ~ Chris

Donna Lofthouse is a wife to Dan, a mother of three, Chris, Austin and Hannah, a mother-in-law to Keila, and Grandma to William. She has five siblings that are very close and her parents are doing well and live near by.

She has enjoyed "making America beautiful" as a licensed hairdresser for many years.

Donna has a love for art which has opened up a river of creativity that flows from and through her. Whether it's creating one of the many unique pieces of silk art, like scarves, prayer shawls, worship flags and banners, or teaching as the Creative Director at GCSSM, Gulf Coast School of Supernatural Ministry, Donna always draws her creativity from God, the One from whom all creativity flows.

She is a two year graduate of GCSSM, which has prepared and equipped her for a leadership role at OFH, Our Fathers House, where she is currently a Director

For the single mothers ministry.

"Where we are leaving a legacy while standing in the Gap for single mothers and their children as they move from testimony to triumph."

Her time volunteering at the Healing Rooms of Manatee over the years has also been very instrumental and equipping. While ministering there, she has delighted in watching others grow in their gifts and finding their true identity in Christ as well as experiencing this growth for herself. The Door, is yet another notable place that she has attributed to the great depth of her inner healing and strengthening as well as developing a more intimate relationship with the Lord. Donna is thankful for all of these opportunities and experiences that have equipped her and prepared her to have the ability to write Austins Harvest.

Receive the Baptism of the Holy Spirit

SALVATION IS A GIFT from God for you. The baptism of the Holy Spirit is another gift He has given to you as well. He's done His part. You have to do your part. What is that? You must receive it! Through the baptism of the Holy Spirit God fills you to overflowing. The evidence of this overflow is your speaking in a language that you did not learn. It's called speaking in tongues.

There are so many benefits to receiving this gift from the Lord. When you pray in tongues, for example, you are praying perfectly because the Holy Spirit gives you the words to say.

In the same way you receive Jesus as your Savior, you ask Him for the baptism of the Holy Spirit and receive it by faith. The Holy Spirit was given on the Day of Pentecost and He is still here! Anyone who is saved is eligible to receive the Holy Spirit. Expect to receive Him when you pray. Expect Him to give you supernatural words. He gives you the utterance, but you have to do the speaking! Don't let fear get in your way.

Father, I have received Jesus as my Lord and Savior. Thank You for saving me. Now I want to receive the gift of the baptism of the Holy Spirit with the evidence of speaking in tongues. I want to walk more closely to You by the Spirit leading me and guiding me. I ask You to fill me with Your Spirit right now to overflowing. Give me the supernatural language You have for me. I receive now! Thank You, Lord!

Acts 1:5
Matthew 3:11
Mark 1:8
Luke 3:16
Luke 24:49
John 1:33
Acts 9:17

Prayer of Forgiveness

THIS IS A GOOD opportunity for you to reflect on your own life and to search your heart for the evidence of unforgiveness or bitterness that you might have been carrying for way too long. If you are willing and ready, just simply write down each name that the Holy Spirit shows you need to forgive and decide to release yourself from the control they have had over your life. This is a three-step process.

Forgiving others, forgiving God and forgiving yourself will be the best thing you could ever do for yourself and for others, and sets you on your path of ultimate freedom and healing. It's easier than you think.

Prayer

Lord Jesus, I repent for holding onto unforgiveness in my heart toward _____.

I repent for all of the bitterness, offenses, resentment, jealousy, retaliation, judgement, and revenge, I also repent for carrying in my heart any and all anger, wrath, rage, accusations, hatred and violence, forgive me if the thought of murder entered my mind or heart toward others. Lord, I choose to forgive them all for what they said or did to me and I no longer hold them accountable for their actions and sins against me. I now break all the sewing and reaping that has taken place in my life that is due to my unforgiveness. As I forgive each person, I pray for God to bless them in every area of their life. Thank you, God, for healing all of those broken places and filling my heart with your peace and your love, the Fathers love.

Father God, I repent for the many times I had blamed you for bad circumstances in my life. Please forgive me for holding unforgiveness in my heart toward you for _____.

I had a false sense of understanding of your plans and motives for my life, I am ready to reconcile my relationship with you again. I no longer hold you accountable and I choose to trust you because you have my best interest at heart. I now break all of the sewing and reaping that has taken place in my life due to my wrong perspective of Who You are to me, my loving Father in Heaven, you provide everything that I will ever need. So yes, I submit myself to you and receive all that you have for me, your love, your peace, your joy and your goodness I thank you in the name of Jesus, Amen.

Finally, I choose to forgive myself, I repent for holding unforgiveness in my heart toward myself for the things that I did or didn't do. _____ and no longer hold myself accountable for my poor choices and sins. I break all of the sewing and reaping that has taken place in my life due to holding unforgiveness toward myself, and I pray many blessings over my life from this day forward. In Jesus name, Amen!

Receive Jesus into your Heart and Invite Him into your Life. Through this opportunity you can be counted as one of "Austin's Harvest."

The Fathers Blessing

The Fathers blessing is an important and intentional prayer that can strengthen the relationship between a father, or respected Father figure and a child of any age. The Fathers Blessing is founded in Biblical truth first seen in the lives of Abraham, Isaac and Jacob foundationally and is a powerful reminder of our heritage and blessing from generation to generation. This prayer is an opportunity to regain/restore a healthy relationship of respect between the two as well as to release the Fathers love and prosperity. This prayer was inspired by Numbers 6:24-26 and from the You-tube video from Elevation Worship with Kari Jobe and Cody Carnes Live from Ballantyne. Watch listen and pray and receive.

Prayer

May the Lord bless you and keep you, The Lord make His face shine upon you and be gracious to you, The Lord lift up His countenance upon you and give you peace. May His favor be upon you and upon your children and all your generations. He is for you- Hallelujah & Amen! Rejoice that He is for you!

Kate's thoughtful gift

Dove release

Author Donna Lofthouse

Austin's Table.

Jack's new guitar

Scavenger hunt and Austin's stone

about us before we were born and he destined us from the beginning to share the likeness of his Son. This means the Son is the oldest among a vast family of brothers and sisters who will become just like him.

"Having determined our destiny ahead of time, he called us to himself and transferred his perfect righteousness to everyone he called. And those who possess his perfect righteousness he co-glorified with his Son!

8:23 The "firstfruits of the Spirit" would include his indwelling presence, his gifts, his wisdom, and his transforming power. Imagine what the full harvest of the Spirit will bring to us! The Aramaic can be translated the awakening of the Spirit."

8:26 The Greek word *huper*-hano is best translated super [or hyper]-intercede for us." We can only imagine how many blessings have come into our lives because of the hyper-intercession of the Holy Spirit.

8:26 Or "groanings." There are three groanings in this chapter. Creation groans for the glorious freedom that is coming (v. 22), we groan to experience the fullness of our status as God's children (v. 23), and the Holy Spirit groans for our complete destiny to be fulfilled (here).

8:27 Or "God, the heart-searcher." God searches our hearts not just to uncover what is wrong, but to fulfill the true desire of our hearts to be fully his. Grace triumphs over judgment.

8:29 The Aramaic can be translated "sealed us" (with God's mark upon us). See also Col. 3:4; Heb. 2:11.

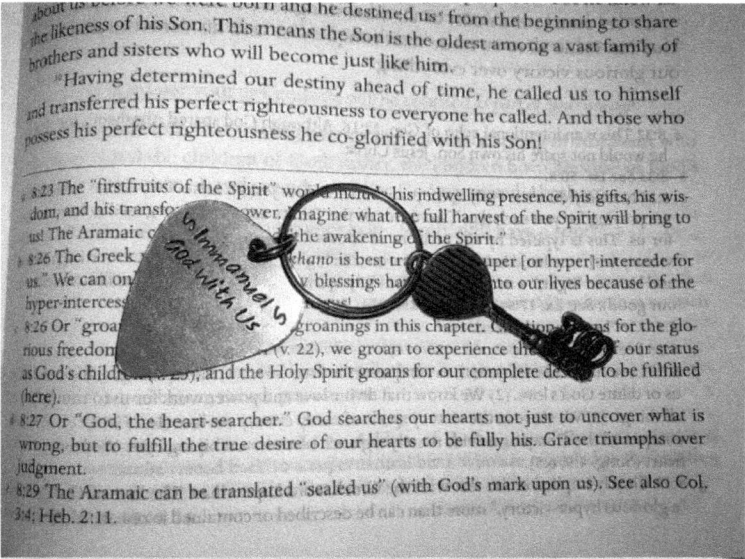

Katrina's gift "Immanuel God with us"

Hannah at 17 with her brother Austin's guitar

Christmas at the Door

Receive Jesus
Into Your Heart

Salvation through Jesus is at the very heart of the life experiences you are about to witness within this book. Without that foundation there would be no testimony to the goodness and love of God. There would be no hope, no joy, no life.

If you have not received Jesus as your Lord and Savior pray this simple prayer with me now.

Dear Heavenly Father, I believe in my heart that Jesus Christ is your son. I believe

He died for me and rose again from the dead for my Salvation. I ask You, Jesus, to come into my heart, to be my Lord and Savior. Thank You for all that you did for me at the cross.

If you've prayed this prayer just now, I celebrate your decision with you! You've started on an amazing journey and you'll never be disappointed in Him.

~ Donna

www.ingramcontent.com/pod-product-compliance
Lightning Source LLC
Chambersburg PA
CBHW030828090426
42737CB00009B/926